Home Equity and Reverse Mortgages

Home Equity and Reverse Mortgages

The Cinderella of the Baby Boomer Retirement

Harlan J. Accola

Please feel free to contact the author with questions and valued feedback. Email is accola4@gmail.com and street address is 8330 County Road Y, Marshfield, WI 54449

Author is a licensed loan officer and NMLS# is 277693

ISBN: 0692044965
ISBN 13: 9780692044964
Library of Congress Control Number: 2017919363
Better Way to Live, Inc., A Marshfield, WI

DEDICATION

This book is dedicated to my wife Brenda —
Without her support, this would never have been
possible. And to our 4 sons, Ben, Josh, Luke, and
Isaac who continue to inspire and impress their
parents more than they could ever realize.

CONTENTS

INTRODUCTION

When Paul Revere made his midnight ride warning the colonists that the "British are coming," it is likely there were more than a few who were irritated about being woken up in the middle of the night and a few who really didn't believe those redcoats were a threat.

This book will warn you that we have a serious retirement problem in this country that will affect old and young alike. Only a few financial advisors, academics, and researchers are talking about it—and more importantly, very few are offering solutions.

The Baby Boomers Are Coming

The baby boomers is a group that is being increasingly ignored in the majority of advertising and news coverage and even ongoing research. It is easy to find news and discussions about the twentysomethings—the "millennials"—but it seems baby boomers are not nearly as fashionable to talk about. Maybe they are just old hat, but baby boomers—those generally defined as being born between 1946 and 1964—have effectively dominated every economic and social trend since they were born. Starting with Gerber baby food and continuing to bell-bottom jeans, Woodstock, the Beatles, miniskirts, station wagons, and minivans, and now ending with erectile dysfunction drugs, Alzheimer's disease, and long-term care issues, baby boomers are still a massive contingent of the population that must be reckoned with.

We are a long way from the "end" of the baby boomers. It is expected that about ten thousand people per day will turn sixty-two for the next twenty years. In 2000, there were thirty-five million people over sixty-five, but in 2030, it is forecast that we will have more than seventy million over sixty-five. Wheelchairs will likely outnumber strollers! The social, medical, political, and economic impact is simply not well understood, and most people are not prepared for the implications.

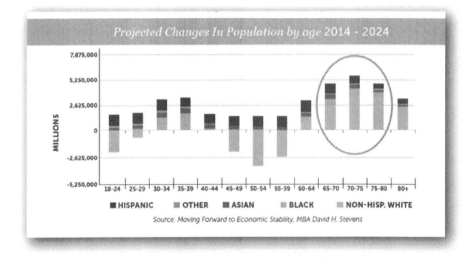

People are living longer, needing more health care and long-term care, spending more, and saving less—and somehow, this is all supposed to come out OK?

Plain and simple, it can't—and it won't—without using a typically scorned and little-used product to activate some of the $6 trillion currently stored in American seniors' home equity. That product is a Home Equity Conversion Mortgage—HECM—the most common reverse mortgage available to those over sixty-two in this country. Yet the vast majority of seniors over sixty-two (and their financial advisors and children) don't want this product and prefer to use it only as a loan of last resort when all other options are exhausted. To date, fewer than five out of one hundred homeowners over sixty-two have taken advantage of this safe and government-insured program.

In an April 2017 CNBC article, Andrew Osterland said, "You don't have to be old, poor, and stupid to get a reverse mortgage."

And that is so true—contrary to very popular opinion. I have been in the reverse mortgage business since 2003, and I have been involved with about one thousand of these loans. The evidence and research clearly show that the best time to get one of these is when you are younger, have money left, and are financially savvy. I have seen their effects on family members, friends, and clients. I have seen their value, resulting in many retirements changed for the better and problems avoided. I plan to get one on my sixty-second birthday.

That is why it is amazing to me that, out of ten thousand people a day turning sixty-two, fewer than two hundred seniors close on a reverse mortgage loan. It doesn't make sense! Like one of my associates, Peter Rueth, said, it's like standing in the middle of a college campus yelling "free beer," and only a couple of people show up.

With overwhelming evidence published in financial journals, why do so many ignore or resist using this valuable financial tool? We will explore the psychology behind those misguided opinions in the pages ahead. But this is bigger than your house or mine—this is about saving retirement as we know it today.

The goal of this book is twofold. First, we are going to investigate the psychology behind why so many seniors are not taking advantage of this clearly safe and economical option. Second, we want this book to create immediate action to use some of the stored $6 trillion of home equity and change the way retirement is done in this country. If you are stuck in the 1960s, when pensions were popular, or in the 1980s, when you could still get 10 or more percent interest on CDs, and you don't want to change or prosper in the next twenty years, then don't read this book. It will require you to think differently from conventional wisdom. It will also force you to change your financial decisions immediately.

The question on the back of my business card is this: If what you thought about money and mortgages was wrong, then when would you want me to tell you?

If you are stretched out on the beach, soaking up the sun and enjoying the day, then this book is designed to wake you up and to tell you about the massive silver tsunami headed your way. It should make you feel uncomfortable and want to do something different with your home and your financial plan than before you picked it up.

Oh, and one more thing—we want to make this somewhat boring and scary subject kind of fun to read about.

So we will start with a fairy tale!

CHAPTER 1

THE CINDERELLA STORY

*Life is what happens to us while
we are making other plans.*
—ALLEN SAUNDERS, AMERICAN WRITER AND CARTOONIST

Cinderella. Who doesn't know this story? This fairy tale dates to ancient Greece and had versions in Asia, Europe, and the Middle East before the Brothers Grimm published it a couple of centuries before Disney put out its famous retelling. It is a wonderful story of how a nobody became a somebody and lived happily ever after. The mean stepsisters did not allow Cinderella to go to the ball—in fact, she was not even supposed to be part of the story. But we all know the prince fell in love with her, as she was the most beautiful girl at the ball. The prince asked her to be his wife and move to the palace, where they lived happily ever after.

Wikipedia (2017) describes the concept this way: "The word 'Cinderella' has, by analogy, come to mean one whose attributes were unrecognized, or *one who unexpectedly achieves recognition or success after a period of obscurity and neglect.*" (Emphasis is mine.)

This story parallels what many in our industry and the financial-planning world see happening to home equity and the reverse mortgage product over the next several years. We believe that the reverse mortgage product will be a major player in helping people live happily ever after. Here is what some experts *outside* our industry and in the financial-planning field are saying: (all bold emphasis are mine)

> Jamie Hopkins, MBA, LLM, the American College of Financial Services and an author of the Retirement Income Certified Professional designation for financial advisors: "The lack of focus on home equity in retirement income planning is **nothing short of a complete failure to properly plan** and utilize all available retirement assets. **This needs to change immediately** because strategic uses of home equity, especially reverse mortgages, could save many people from financial failure in retirement and **help stem the overall retirement income crisis** facing Americans" (Hopkins— Forbes Magazine Oct 7, 2016: Reverse Mortgages Can Be A Retiree's Saving Grace

> Robert Merton, Nobel Prize–winning economist: "Americans have wrongly steered clear of reverse mortgages. This needs to change. Individuals and industry leaders need to better understand how reverse mortgages can be effectively used. **A more**

widespread and better understanding of reverse mortgage strategies needs to occur in order to better serve America's senior population and retirees."

Wade Pfau, PhD, Professor of Retirement Income, The American College: "Through inertia and stubbornness, old ideas die slowly. Financial advisors maintain a dismal view about reverse mortgages. However, much has changed in just the past few years. **Revisit your outdated thinking with an open mind** about a tool that is on the cusp of more widespread use" (Pfau 2015).

It's simple: no matter how good a job financial advisors do, there is not enough money out there to get all the baby boomers to life expectancy, and those who do have enough money may have it all wiped out at the end with health care or high taxes to take care of those who didn't save. It is going to affect everyone unless we do something different now. If you think you are safe, then take a look at what would happen if you live to be ninety-five. What if your spouse dies early or one of you has a devastating and expensive illness? Life is what happens while you are planning other things. The only thing certain about the future is that it is uncertain.

There are really two groups—people who need a reverse mortgage now if they want to have a more comfortable retirement and those who think they will do just fine without one because they have saved quite a bit. The fact is that both groups will have a better retirement and a higher net worth if they do a reverse mortgage as early as sixty-two.

We recommend that you read the research on financial planning and reverse mortgages since 2012. Most of it was published in the respected *Journal of Financial Planning*, which carries only peer-reviewed articles. A partial list of researchers in the financial-planning space who have all come to this same conclusion can be found in appendix 1. This list was compiled from toolsforretirementplanning.com, where you can find even more resources.

A concise summary of all the research conducted to date can be found in chapter 6 of Wade Pfau's book, *Reverse Mortgages: How to Use Reverse Mortgages to Secure Your Retirement* (2016). This landmark reference book can and should be used to do exactly what the title says: to secure your retirement. If you want a completely unbiased, academic, and well-researched view of reverse mortgages, then this is the book to read. In the book's preface, Pfau says, "Readers can be confident that I do not receive any financial gain from the sale of reverse mortgages. I'm writing from outside the reverse mortgage industry. My overarching interest is in building efficient retirement income plans" (ix).

This Cinderella solution mirrors the title of the *TIME* magazine article "Retirees' Biggest Asset May Be Hiding in Plain Sight" (Kadlec 2016). It can increase cash flow in retirement, save money in income taxes, and increase your net worth at death, thus leaving a larger legacy.

Let's stand outside a grocery store with a checklist and ask everyone with a tint of gray in his or her hair this question: "Would you like to have more cash flow in retirement, pay lower income taxes, and have a higher net worth and thus a greater legacy to pass on to your heirs?"

My guess is that almost everyone would say yes. But when we follow it up with this advice, the response may change: "Then you should get a reverse mortgage as soon as you turn sixty-two."

"Oh, I don't want one of them!"

Yep, everyone wants to go to heaven, but nobody wants to die.

The story is written: the girl in rags will become queen. It's just a matter of time.

Part of the $6 trillion in home equity released by HECM reverse mortgages is going to become the Cinderella of retirement income in the future. Why isn't it now?

Baby boomers know the Bon Jovi song "You Give Love a Bad Name." Why do reverse mortgages have a bad name?

It is important to note here that this book will interchangeably refer to reverse mortgages and HECMs as the same product. There are some non—-FHA (Federal Housing Administration) mortgages that are not insured by the US Department of Housing and Urban Development (HUD), and those will not be discussed in this book because they do not have the same protections and guarantees.

Why is the reverse mortgage a neglected and obscure retirement tool? It is mostly psychological. But perception is reality for millions of retirees. How did the reverse mortgage product get a bad name? There are perhaps many answers to this question, but the primary one is it was originally sold and marketed (and still is by many companies) as the loan of last resort. If you are broke, have no other options, and need money, then maybe—just maybe—you want to look into a reverse mortgage. This reputation will literally take years to change and is one of the main reasons I am writing this book. We must change this thought process if we want to change to a better retirement.

Depression-Era Thinking

The greatest generation—my parents—told us baby boomers about the Great Depression. People lost their houses and farms because of mortgages. In the 1960s, 1970s, and 1980s, mortgage-burning parties celebrating the final payoff on a mortgage were commonplace, and this practice even made it into an episode of *All in the Family* in 1975. During the Depression era, mortgages were much riskier, and if you fell behind, then you could indeed lose your home. There were no Fannie Mae thirty-year mortgages or FHA HECM reverse mortgages guaranteed up to age 150. Unfortunately, this goal of a "free-and-clear" home has become outdated almost a century after the Great Depression. Research shows that a free-and-clear home can be inefficient and, in some cases, unsafe. You will have less cash available and a lower net worth by locking up all your equity in your house. From a safety perspective, a reverse mortgage is non-recourse and guarantees borrowers can stay in their homes for the rest of their lives as long as they live there and pay taxes and insurance, just like they would if their homes were paid off. Equity is often more highly valued than cash, but cash is the most important financial ingredient in retirement. You can't use equity to buy gas and groceries—more on that later.

Foreclosures and Widows

Related to Depression-era thinking is the widespread national media attention on foreclosures that happened for two reasons. The first reason was the tax and insurance defaults that happened when people in the program who took out a reverse mortgage could not keep up with their real-estate taxes. They would have lost their homes anyway because the county would have foreclosed, but the reverse mortgages were blamed. Lenders are required to file foreclosure by the FHA, which insures the product if the taxes are not paid. Several rules have changed to prevent those loans from being done in the first place.

But perhaps the worst thing that ever happened to the reverse mortgage program is the nonborrowing-spouse debacle. Prior to 2014, an older spouse, usually the husband, was able to remove his underage wife (under sixty-two) from the title and then take out the reverse mortgage; together, they would spend the money and live happily ever after— that is, until he passed away. Then the loan was due because his wife was not part of the loan. She was not old enough when the loan was done. Several of these situations happened after the 2008 housing crash. AARP caught wind of some widows being foreclosed on, and its attorneys joined the widows in a lawsuit against HUD and Wells Fargo. The case was fought in the court of public opinion as much as in the regular courts. It was one of the worst public-relations debacles for the reverse mortgage industry. If you want to look bad from a public-relations standpoint, then simply have your product repeatedly characterized as foreclosing on widows on the front pages of newspapers and in TV programs across the country. (Bear in mind that all the widows involved in the court case had signed off on the houses and had no right to stay there because of their decisions years before.) The court case was eventually settled, and the FHA changed the rules for every HECM reverse mortgage going forward. Now if you have an underage spouse, then you are allowed to do the loan and include your underage husband or wife as part of the guarantee that both of you can stay in the home for as long as you wish, no matter who passes away first. Although this rule has changed and underage spouses are now protected, we will still hear about this unfortunate problem for many years to come. It is a dark chapter that will not go away soon. But your underage spouse will not be kicked out of the home after your death (assuming you are still married) on a new loan you originate today, period. (In Texas, both spouses must be over sixty-two.)

Misuses of Reverse Mortgages

As with any product, there are unscrupulous characters, either loan officers, financial advisors, or contractors, who would take advantage of trusting seniors by misusing equity proceeds. However, newer and stronger regulations by the FHA and other regulatory agencies make it very difficult to defraud this very trusting and protected class.

We cover other negative issues and explain them throughout this book. But it is important to note that reverse mortgages are similar to Cinderella—because of her reputation as a humble kitchen maid, no one thought she could be the queen of the kingdom. Things are not always as they seem, and those with an open mind will find a far different product from the image that exists in conventional wisdom.

No one ever thought Cinderella was really the beautiful young lady at the ball until the glass slipper fit. Let's try on an HECM for a baby boomer retirement and see how it fits.

CHAPTER 2

THE CURRENT STATE OF THE KINGDOM

The future is now. It's time to grow up and be strong. Tomorrow may well be too late.
—NEIL LABUTE, AMERICAN FILM DIRECTOR

If I got lost coming to your house and called you for directions, then the first question you would ask me is "Where are you?" Cinderella not only knew where she was but also where she had to go. What is the situation in the kingdom you are living in today—and more importantly—what does it look like in the future?

In Cinderella's story, some versions tell of a rat turned into a coachman. There is a rat in the baby boomer story too. It is the bulge of the rat going through the snake for the last seventy-plus years. Don't forget: ten thousand people per day are turning sixty-two for the next couple of decades. This has never happened in any country—ever! We are in uncharted waters.

And this is all happening as people are living longer in the kingdom, have fewer pensions, fewer savings, higher medical costs, all-time-low interest rates, more spending, more Alzheimer's disease, more, more, more—all hitting us at the wrong time. The skin of the snake—our economic system—can expand only so much before there are problems. We can't ignore the undeniable statistics.

Let's start with the biggest and most important issue in retirement in this country—social security.

Although politicians have largely ignored the silver tsunami, President Bush did highlight the social security problem in his 2005 State of the Union address: "In today's world, people are living longer and therefore drawing benefits longer—and those benefits are scheduled to rise dramatically over the next few decades. *And instead of sixteen workers paying in for every beneficiary, right now it's only about three workers*—and over the next few decades, that number will fall to just two workers per beneficiary. With each passing year, fewer workers are paying ever-higher benefits to an ever-larger number of retirees" (US Department of State 2005, emphasis added).

Social security is not the only issue. What about low savings rates, increasing health-care costs, and long-term care? The purpose of this book is not to reiterate all the statistical analyses about this problem. That has already been done by far more capable writers, and I encourage you to read their work. *The Coming Generational Storm* (2004) and *The Clash of Generations* (2012), coauthored by Laurence Kotlikoff and Scott Burns, and *Falling Short: The Coming Retirement Crisis and What to Do about It* (2014), by Charles Ellis, Alicia Munnell, and Andrew Eschtruth, clearly lay out the issues, concerns, and warnings that should be more widely broadcast.

Here are ten statistics that will give you a very good idea of the crisis we are facing over the next couple of decades (Backman 2017):

1. **Living longer.** One out of every four people over sixty-five will live past ninety years old. Not even half of those over sixty-five have enough funds to make it past ninety.
2. **Not enough savings.** One out of three have no retirement savings at all, and more than half have less than $10,000.
3. **Overdependence on social security.** For 40 percent of single seniors over sixty-five, at least 90 percent of their income comes from social security.
4. **Confidence crisis.** Only about half of Americans think they're saving enough.
5. **Working longer.** Over one-third of retirees expect to work in retirement.
6. **Outliving savings**. Over 60 percent of baby boomers are more worried about running out of money than about dying.
7. **No plans for fun.** About 60 percent of retirees don't budget for vacations or other fun things.
8. **High cost of health care.** The average healthy couple will spend almost $400,000 on health care during retirement.
9. **Spending more.** About half of retired households are spending more money, not less, in retirement.
10. **Bankruptcy?** Seniors are the fastest-growing group of bankruptcy filers in the country.

I could fill this book with scary statistics that would make you worry more than what is necessary. This book is not designed to put you into a sad state but simply to let you know there is not enough money to fund retirement the way it has been done in the past. If everyone had a bag full of gold coins stored away in a drawer in their kitchens, then it would certainly change the way they look at retirement. The truth is, for millions of homeowners, something as good and as valuable as those gold coins is stored in their homes in the form of $6 trillion in home equity. Let's put that into perspective. Outstanding auto loans are only about a trillion. The student loan industry that we hear so much about is only $1 trillion, and the huge credit card industry is only about $800 billion. *Only*—yes, those are really big numbers, but they seem smaller in comparison to home equity, and those numbers are growing every day. By 2022, the National Reverse Mortgage Lenders Association (NRMLA) projects home equity to be more than $8 trillion in homes owned by seniors over the age of sixty-two. If only part of that wealth was used to fund retirement longevity, then the kingdom would be a brighter and safer place financially.

There are many retirees who feel this only affects other people. It is true that you may be better off than your neighbor or your friends, but what if you live to be ninety-five, especially if you are single for part of that time? And even if you are fine, then what will happen to taxes when millions of other baby boomers need health care, long-term care, food stamps, and the like? You will be forced to share your nest egg every time you pull money from your IRA or earnings from your investments. This affects everyone in the kingdom!

Isn't the Government Taking Care of This?

Politically, both parties have accused the other of not taking care of the elderly. Pushing Grandma off the cliff was the subject of more than a few political cartoons. But the truth is that neither party has a good plan to deal with this. They are sitting on the beach as well and not doing anything about the tsunami that is coming ashore. Cinderella didn't wait for something to happen at the castle. She did what she could in her own house. We need to make plans to weather the storm. There is nothing wrong with encouraging our representatives in Washington to do something about the problems in the kingdom. But most of us know that waiting for Washington is likely not the best solution. We need to do something ourselves. The next chapter gives you a glimpse into the future of how two baby boomers could end up.

CHAPTER 3

THE TALE OF TWO WIDOWS

*It's not the things we don't know
that get us into trouble;
it's the things we know that ain't so.*
—WILL ROGERS, ACTOR, COWBOY, HUMORIST,
NEWSPAPER COLUMNIST, ETC.

In the fairy tale, Cinderella's stepmom may have found a husband who would take care of her and her two mean daughters, but most of the time, things don't work out that way. One of the main reasons I am in this business is because of the huge need for couples to make plans now so that when the wife becomes a widow down the road, she will not be in poverty. What baby boomer husbands do today will determine how well their brides will be taken care of when they are gone.

At a recent NRMLA conference, Linda K. Stone from the Women's Institute for a Secure Retirement (wiserwomen. org) shared some shocking statistics about widows:

- There are six million more women than men over age sixty-five.

- There are 1.9 million more women at age eighty-five.
- At age eighty-five and older, 71 percent are women.

Thus, they are the most likely group to end up in poverty, even though they have never been there before. This creates a perfect storm for women: they earn less, take more time away from work, do more part-time work, have less in savings and pensions, live longer, and live alone in retirement. They also have more financial risks: inflation, death of a spouse, health-care costs, and outliving assets.

- Currently, 20 percent of women over sixty-five are in poverty, and that number is increasing.
- Most live only on social security.
- Fifty percent live into their nineties, while only 30 percent of men make it into their nineties.
- Women are four times more likely to outlive their spouses.
- Eighty-five percent of people over eighty-five are widows.
- After a spouse's death, income usually decreases by 40 percent because only one social security check continues.
- Half of women over sixty-five are single.

If you are married – you need to take care of your spouse. This is about taking care of your family and your surviving spouse. As a husband, it is more likely you will pass first, and decisions you make regarding your finances and your home will determine whether your wife will live in poverty as a widow, even if as a couple you have never been there before. Most people plan as a couple, not as a single, but what if?

Let's look at two couples: Diane and Bob and Linda and David. They live next door to one another in similarly valued homes in a nice neighborhood. Bob and David both retired at the same time from the same company. Bob drew social security at sixty-two—in fact, he signed up the same day he retired. David decided to wait, took out a reverse mortgage, and took payments from sixty-two to seventy from the reverse mortgage to supplement the money they were not getting in social security. (See note at the end of this chapter.) All four of them worked part time for "fun money." Bob's monthly social security was $1,500, and by the time David got to seventy, his monthly social security was more than $2,600. When they went on vacation together or bought new cars, they both would draw money out of their IRAs, but Bob paid more in taxes most years because his social security, IRA, and part-time income created more income taxes. David's income from the HECM was not taxable, so when he drew money out of the IRA, he didn't need as much because he paid very little or nothing in taxes.

After enjoying more than two decades of retirement, both David and Bob died at eighty-five. Now it wasn't David and Bob, it was just Diane and Linda. Linda's social security check was almost double Diane's, and she had more money left in her IRA. Every time she drew it out, she would make payments to her HECM line of credit and receive a tax deduction on the interest that had accrued. Almost all of her IRA ended up coming out tax-free. Diane could not make ends meet on her drastically reduced income. She asked Linda about her HECM, which Bob always said was a dumb idea. Linda told her about the program, but it had changed dramatically in twenty years. Because her real-estate taxes had increased and the IRA was mostly gone, Diane could not qualify on her own anymore. Now she would need to decide whether to borrow on her credit cards to keep things going or to sell her home before she got behind on taxes. Most of her remaining assets were stuck in illiquid home equity.

Of course, this is a very general and oversimplified example. Many numbers and Excel spreadsheets would need to be run to prove all the details in this scenario that Linda would be better off than Diane. But research has already been conducted by respected financial-planning academics (listed in chapter 1) proving that couples—and especially widows—are better off *if* a reverse mortgage is used right at the beginning of retirement as part of a coordinated financial retirement plan instead of as a loan of last resort.

If you are retired or planning to do soon, then do you want to make decisions about a reverse mortgage with calculated, well-researched facts, or would you rather use outdated and incorrect hearsay from people who have never looked into the numbers? For example, Dave Ramsey and other radio personalities who have done zero research and have no licenses and qualifications, except as entertainers, have spoken out against reverse mortgages. They have proliferated incorrect assumptions and scared people away with basic untruths. The research by independent third parties is solid. Read it before (or after) you listen to your brother-in-law or Dave Ramsey.

No one ever expected Cinderella to be the prince's wife, but that is what happened. Your future self or your spouse will thank you for making the right decision early in retirement on the proper way to use home equity. "As a husband and father, I want to appeal to other husbands and fathers. As a husband, I believe it is my responsibility to care for and provide for my wife, whom I exchanged vows with many years ago. I expect many of you will feel the same way. My spouse is my strength, my partner, helped raise our children, and supported my career through thick and thin, often at the expense of her own goals. As a male, I want to appeal to other husbands to think about proper planning if you pass first. I would consider it a tragedy if I passed away and left her with a situation that would cause her to live the last part of her life in poverty because of the choices I made that she trusted me with while we were a couple. The proper use or misuse—or nonuse—of our home equity is a major part of those decisions. Don't ignore a large part of the wealth you have accumulated together, and don't make the mistake that most husbands are making—ignoring home equity to the expense of their wives' futures and financial safety. That is not happily ever after—it's not a fairy-tale ending!

CHAPTER 4

THE SWISS ARMY KNIFE

It is unique. There are no other financial tools like it!
DAN HULTQUIST, UNDERSTANDING REVERSE AUTHOR

So far in this book, we have talked in detail about the concept of reverse mortgages as a neglected and over-looked solution to our country's retirement crisis. I assumed that the reader picking up this book already knew some-thing about the details of a reverse mortgage, but I think it's important that some of the basics are covered in this chap-ter. For an in-depth understanding of the product and how it works, the best book to read—by far—is Dan Hultquist's *Understanding Reverse* (20–), which is revised each year to reflect changes in the product and qualifications. It is im-portant to get the most recent edition as there were major changes made to the program on October 2nd of 2017. In this chapter, I will provide a brief explanation of an HECM reverse mortgage, how you qualify, and how it works.

What It Is

An HECM is nothing more than a regular mortgage that has a very unusual repayment program. You are able to receive between 30 and 75 percent of the value of your home based on current interest rates and your age. First things first: there is a fairy godmother, and her name is FHA. Quite frankly, I would not be interested in a reverse mortgage for myself or anyone else unless the fairy godmother, the FHA mortgage insurance program, was not backing up the guarantees of this very safe but unusual loan. (More on that in chapter 10.) There are two important guarantees. First, the FHA backs up the lender guarantee that no payments are required until after you permanently move out of the house, which is usually a year after you are dead! The second guarantee means that only home equity is responsible for the loan—not you, your heirs, your estate, your trust, or any other asset you own. This cannot be overstated. For virtually every other loan or mortgage you have ever taken out, you signed a personal guarantee. At a reverse mortgage signing, you will sign a "Release of Personal Liability" form. Only the house equity is responsible for paying the loan back, and if it doesn't have enough money at the end, then the FHA mortgage insurance pays it back. The mortgages that you are used to, a typical forward mortgage, are due monthly and have a specific time period, such as fifteen or thirty years, for you to pay the money back. I think everyone would agree that not having to pay this loan back until the year after you are permanently out of the home is really a very good deal. I doubt you have any other loans that are due a year after you are dead!

Paying It Back

Payments during your lifetime while you are living in the house are optional. So many people think you're not allowed to make payments on a reverse mortgage. That is not true! Payments are optional and flexible with a reverse mortgage. If you wish to make monthly payments, annual payments, or occasional larger payments, then you can do that. And many borrowers do just that to manage cash flow, equity, or tax deductions.

What happens after you die? Remember, you still own the house, as you never gave up ownership in the beginning. Now, the loan will need to be either paid off or refinanced like any other mortgage. If the house is sold, as is most often the case, and there is equity left in the home, then your heirs would receive the remaining equity. But if you lived a long time, home prices were down the year you passed away, and more was owed on the house than what it was worth, then the difference that is owed is not your or your estate's responsibility. The bill would go to the FHA mortgage insurance. So if it's good, then the money goes to your children, and if it's bad, then the FHA mortgage insurance pays the difference. You are not guaranteed to win, but you and your family are guaranteed never to lose more than the home equity you have pledged.

How Do You Qualify?

New rules have been put in place within the last couple of years to avoid foreclosures because of tax and insurance defaults. So although it is harder to qualify now than in the past, it is still easier to qualify for a reverse mortgage as compared to a forward mortgage. First, either you or your spouse must be over sixty-two. (In Texas, both of you must be older than sixty-two.) Second, the loan must be on a home that is your primary residence that is FHA qualified. That would include most manufactured homes built after 1976 and condos that are specifically approved by the FHA. You can even mortgage a home that is up to four units as long as the landlord is living in one of the units. Your credit and income must be good enough to prove that you are able and willing to pay real estate taxes and insurance for the foreseeable future. If you are purchasing a home, then there are a few other qualifications, and you will be required to have a down payment equivalent to 25 to 60 percent of the home value, depending on your age. Of course, the older you are, the less money you'd be required to put down.

How They Work

When I present in front of a group and try to briefly explain how a reverse mortgage works, I pull my red Swiss Army knife from my pocket—provided it was not taken away by

the TSA screening at the last airport because it was acciden-
tally in my carry-on luggage! Here is an interesting piece of
trivia: unfortunately, Cinderella would not have been able to
have a Swiss Army knife because they weren't invented by
the Swiss until 1884, and the Brothers Grimm published the
story in 1812.

There are four primary tools that can be unfolded from the
reverse mortgage Swiss Army knife.

Tool 1: Lump-Sum Payment

The first is a lump sum. The lump sum is typically used to pay
off an existing mortgage or to purchase a retirement home
when downsizing or upsizing. Let's stop here for a second
and talk about having a mortgage payment in retirement.
Housing expenses, especially mortgage payments, are
a big threat to your retirement income and assets. Those
costs are typically the largest retirement costs. About one
third of people over sixty-two are still making mortgage
payments when they don't have to. If you and your financial advisor look at your situation and you are over sixty-
two, have about 50 percent equity, and are still making a
mortgage payment, then it will rarely make sense for you
to continue doing that. This tool that helps that group is
perhaps the most important tool in averting the retirement
crisis facing the baby boomers. Many people have told me,
"But my mortgage payment is only a thousand a month."
That's not really true. It's $12,000 per year and $120,000
over the first ten years of retirement. Making a mortgage

payment and creating more equity when you don't need it is a luxury most people cannot afford. Even if you can afford to make mortgage payments ten, twenty, or thirty years into retirement, it's not the most efficient use of your cash flow, tax and estate planning, and overall net worth.

Dr. Barry Sacks, who has done research for years on the HECM product, in a recent webinar conversation I had with him used the word "dangerous" when talking about making mortgage payments in retirement when you could have a reverse mortgage.

Reverse Mortgages for Purchase

The same issue applies when you buy a home. Let's say you're purchasing a $400,000 home as your final retirement home. If you put down only 20 percent, then you will pay about $550,000 for the next thirty years on a regular mortgage PLUS the original $80,000 down payment. If you pay cash, then you will have to come up with $400,000. If you do a reverse mortgage in your 70s, for example, then you'll have to come up with roughly $200,000 one time, and you are done making mortgage payments on the house for the rest of your life unless you want to. Lump-sum payments can also be used to pay off other debts that require payments, such as credit cards or cars, or to make aging-in-place improvements to your house. With a lump sum at sixty two, you will be able to access about $160,000 for purchasing or refinancing. Go to Chapter 12 to learn more about using a reverse for purchase to finance your new retirement home!

Tool 2: The Reverse Line of Credit HECM LOC

The second blade or tool from the Swiss Army knife is perhaps the most exciting, unusual, and hard-to-understand concept in the whole reverse mortgage world. It is a line of credit. Most people think they're familiar with a HELOC (home equity line of credit), but we call this a HECM LOC (home equity conversion mortgage line of credit), and it's very different. A regular HELOC requires monthly payments, does not grow, and can be called due at any time. It may be free or very inexpensive, but it is not designed for people in retirement. A HECM LOC is used to convert equity into cash without requiring you to make payments and to convert cash back into equity at a time in your life when it doesn't make any sense or is hard to do so. Perhaps the most dangerous part of the HELOC is that it can be called at any time and is usually required to change into repayment status after five or ten years. Then a much higher payment is required as compared to interest-only payments at the beginning. All the payments on a HECM LOC are optional (except after you move out or pass away), and *you* choose when and how much they are going to be.

But here is the biggest reason why you want a HECM LOC in retirement: it has a guaranteed growth factor for as long as you live in the home, no matter what. If the value of the home goes down, the stock market crashes, interest rates skyrocket, or the economy is awful, then the available amount of your equity will continue to grow every year between 4 and 6 percent— based on current rates— no matter what happens. It's always wise to get an umbrella before it starts to rain. It is simply smart to create an available line of credit before you actually need it. Maybe you're still working at sixty-two. Maybe you like having your house paid off. Maybe you have lots of money in your retirement account. Maybe you're close to having your house completely paid off. Regardless of all those things, the experts agree that it is wise to put a growing reverse mortgage line of credit on your home as soon as you are eligible. As we have said many times, the only thing certain about the future is that it is uncertain. When health changes, when your investments change, when someone passes, when some positive opportunity pops up, or when you simply want to help out a child or grandchild or maybe do that bucket-list vacation, the HECM LOC is there, larger than it was the day you took it out. Remember, the equity in your house is worthless until it is converted to cash. You can't use your front steps to buy gas, and you can't rip off the screen door and take it to the grocery store. There are only two ways to convert your home equity into cash. One is to sell the home, but then you have to move. The other is to take out a loan, which usually requires payments. But in the case of a reverse mortgage line of credit, that equity will be immediately available to you whenever you need it or want it. The peace of mind that comes from knowing money is available no matter what is in your future is hard to place a value on. In fact, even your closing costs are paid for with future home equity—not with cash today.

Tool 3: Monthly Payments

The third tool is a reverse monthly payment. Just think of the thousands—no, the tens of thousands—of dollars in payments you have made on your house. It isn't that un-usual to think that your house would make payments back to you because of all the payments you have made on it. Depending on your age and the value of your home, your reverse mortgage lender will give you options for how much you can receive in payments over a specific period of time. For example, maybe you're eligible to receive $1,500 per month for the rest of your life, $2,000 a month for the next twelve years, or $3,000 a month for the next five years. Each situation is different and will change depending on your age and home value. These payments are guaranteed regardless of your home's value for as long as you or your spouse lives in the home.

Tool 4: Combination

The fourth tool is just a combination of the previous three tools. Let's say that you have a $400,000 home with a $50,000 remaining mortgage balance. You could use a lump sum to pay off the existing mortgage, take out the $100,000 credit line that would grow at about 5 percent per year, and then have a $500-per-month payment. That monthly payment comes just like a social security check every month for the rest of your life as long as you live in the home. The great thing is that you can change these options without refinanc-ing your loan as your needs change. If the value of your house goes down, then the FHA mortgage insurance guar-antees the original payments from the loan. If the value of your house goes up, you can refinance and get more cash out or a larger credit line or larger monthly checks.

The purpose of using one or all of these tools from the reverse Swiss Army knife simply creates spendable and liquid cash out of perhaps your largest asset. This is far more powerful than you realize until you put it to work. It literally changes the way you plan financially and live during retirement.

See appendix 2 for more resources on how the formulas and mechanics of a reverse mortgage work.

In the next chapter, we put all this together with a very personal story of how reverse mortgages work with your other assets in the story of the three buckets—and this is *not* a fairy tale; it's real life.

CHAPTER 5

THE THREE BUCKETS

*Sometimes the questions are complicated
and the answers are simple.*
—Dr. Seuss

What does dairy farming have to do with explaining a reverse mortgage loan to your clients? I grew up on a dairy farm in Wisconsin, and even though I have not milked a cow since I was eighteen, I've found that this story is a great way to communicate with my clients. I rarely speak to a client or financial planner without showing the following illustration of the three buckets. I don't know if Cinderella worked on a farm, but I'm pretty sure that she lived in the country, so I think this fits with her story as well. This story actually started because of a discussion I had with my then-sixteen-year-old son, Isaac, several years ago. The buckets that I'm talking about are not filled with milk but with financial assets.

One sunny spring afternoon, Isaac, our youngest of four sons, came home and overheard me and my wife talking about an anonymous client I had helped with a reverse mortgage that day. He paused for a minute in the kitchen on the way out to play basketball in the driveway. "Hey, Dad," he said. "Those reverse mortgages you do for the old people? I guess it's pretty nice for them because they buy houses and go on trips and get money, but those things really rip off the kids, don't they?"

I was shocked. Any father would want his sons to be impressed with the kind of work they did. Obviously, Isaac didn't feel that way. I was also surprised my sixteen-year-old had a strong opinion about it. "Why do you think that?" I asked.

"Well, I've talked to my big brothers about this. As an attorney, oldest brother Ben doesn't think it's a good deal. And Josh, he's a smart engineer, and he's not impressed with them either."

I said, "Have you talked to your third brother, Luke? What did he say?" Luke works in commercial lending for a large bank.

Isaac said, "He doesn't think they're a good idea either because if they were good, then the big banks would be selling them."

I was kind of devastated, but then it got worse. He said, "That's OK, Dad. We understand you have to make a living, but you and Mom aren't going to get one of these when you get older on this house, are you?"

I guess it was OK for me to play Robin Hood and rip off all the other millennials and give to the old people, but I had to at least spare the four of them. I said, "Yes, Isaac. We are going to get one of these the day we turn sixty-two, which is not only good for us but also for you and your brothers."

I began my explanation by drawing three circles and two rectangles on a legal pad, as in the following illustration.

The first bucket represents monthly income, such as social security payments, wages, and pension income. The second bucket represents retirement savings or the nest egg—a lump sum of everything from savings accounts, IRAs, CDs, 401(k)s, and 403(b)s to change jars and gold coins. The income value of this bucket is harder to determine, but this bucket spins off a certain amount of income when needed, either in interest and dividends or by simply cashing in the principal. This money may have been put away years ago and was designed to be spent in retirement. Retirees' biggest fear is that they'll outlive the life of this bucket. Financial professionals spend almost 99 percent of their time analyzing, projecting, sifting, calculating, and recalculating the value and use of the first two buckets but rarely consider the third bucket.

At this point, Isaac interrupted me and said, "I understand all about the second bucket because I talked to Jason, your financial advisor who comes here and helps you invest bucket two."

Then he verbalized what everyone thinks, including most financial advisors: "Why can't you use the money in bucket two instead of doing a reverse mortgage? Because if Jason does his job, then you won't need to worry about the money in the house. "

The fact is that most people don't have enough money in bucket two for the financial advisor to manage until age ninety, and even if they do, then it is more efficiently used, according to the research, if home equity is part of the planning.

I said, "Isaac, think about this. Our house payment is two thousand dollars per month." I pulled out a one hundred dollar bill, which helps keep the attention of a sixteen-year-old. "We deposit twenty of these one hundred dollar bills every single month into bucket three. But as we put money into our home, something strange happens. It turns into equity, and only two people can turn that equity back into cash."

Isaac said, "I know that would be you and Mom."

"No," I said. "It belongs to us, but we are not in charge of turning that equity back to cash. Only a buyer who is willing to purchase our home and to give us cash for the equity in our home or a mortgage lender who, after lots of paper, decides to give us a certain amount of our equity back in the form of cash can do that. As soon as that mortgage lender gives us that cash, he or she will ask us to pay it back starting the very next month, turning cash back into equity, which defeats the whole purpose of having cash in retirement. So many people place such a high value on equity, which is good, but cash is far better in our retirement years. Equity cannot be accurately valued until you sell, and equity cannot be used until it is converted to cash. It's like having a big chunk of cash in our living room in an unbreakable glass case. We can look at it, but we can't use it."

Interestingly enough, depending on a client's other assets, the third bucket is usually valued at 30 to 50 percent of a client's total net worth. Yet most financial professionals—as well as our four sons—largely ignore bucket three.

As reverse mortgage professionals, we spend the majority of our time on bucket three; however, I spend a significant amount of time explaining to my clients that, for qualified borrowers aged sixty-two and older, their homes are fungible—that is, a significant portion of the equity in their homes can be reduced to dollars. Clients must be able to understand the fundamental difference between their *homes*, perhaps the most intimate object of their financial lives, and their *house equity*. The fact that we live in this asset dramatically affects our attitude toward using it as a retirement tool. But we can't take it with us, and sooner or later, our house will be liquidated and denominated into dollars, just like our IRAs.

I explained these basic things about equity to Isaac using a fake one hundred dollar bill and a real one hundred dollar bill. The difference between equity and cash is a difficult thing for anyone to understand, whether you're sixteen, sixty-two, or ninety-two. I explained to Isaac that when his mother and I turn sixty-two, we will be getting a reverse mortgage and converting that equity to cash. We will be following the research that has been done by the people in the financial-planning community who are much smarter than we are. We will be better stewards of our wealth by spending some of the money in bucket three right away in the beginning of retirement and preserving the assets in bucket two. Ultimately, there is really no difference between the three buckets. They all have money put into them when we have extra, and when we need to take money out for expenses in retirement, we have to convert those deposits into withdrawals. Unfortunately, because we live in the bucket-three asset, it becomes a very difficult mental issue to convert that equity into cash and to take income from that bucket.

Because of this psychological brick wall, many clients refuse to even consider their home equity as a source of cash flow and choose instead to use it as a retirement drain. (See the two arrows by the third bucket, as they can go either way.) The typical retiree takes money out of the first two buckets to fund the third bucket. They pay taxes, insurance, maintenance, and often, a continued monthly house payment when they are well past the age of sixty-two. With a reverse mortgage loan, reverse mortgage borrowers no longer have to do that using buckets one and two, although tax, insurance, and maintenance payments are always required. How many retirees are still contributing to IRAs? Very few. But how many are still contributing to bucket three and plan to do so until the end of their lives in their homes? Most of them. They either make payments, or if the house is paid off, continue to put money into the house in the form of maintenance, taxes, and insurance.

Why do retirees and their advisors have no problem with taking money out of the IRA or savings account to fund retirement cash flow, yet when we suggest a reverse mortgage, they decide to wait until bucket two is empty before calling us? After all, they put money into the second bucket so they would have something when they retired. We must remind our clients that they also have religiously put money into their homes in the form of payments, improvements, taxes, and the like. In its simplest form, a reverse mortgage is nothing more than a tool that turns home equity back into cash without affecting your ability to live in your home. It allows you to withdraw money from bucket three instead of continuing to contribute to it.

I have used this simple drawing to help my clients and their advisors overcome the psychological barrier of withdrawing money from the third bucket. Of course, there is still one argument that comes up often: what about the heirs?

Perhaps that was part of the concern that Isaac and his brothers had. But I know our sons, and greed was not the motivating factor. It was really more of a worry that we were doing something wrong that really didn't make sense financially. Perhaps we were making a foolish decision. Quite frankly, there are many financial advisors (and relatives) who think that anyone who gets a reverse mortgage is making a foolish decision. That is the concern that most children have. Another chapter will address the desire that most parents have, which is to pass on their home to their children free and clear. But first, let's look at how the three buckets affect the heirs.

Heirs should always be more concerned about Mom and Dad's need for money first, and they usually are. I saw a sign outside a church several years ago that read: "The cost of living is high, but it is still extremely popular." *Thus, the only way you can leave more money for your heirs is if you die early.* Very few children hope that you die early so that they get more money. Think about it: as soon as you retire and less money is going into bucket one, you must start drawing from either bucket two or bucket three. If you take money from the third bucket, then there will be less home equity for the heirs, especially once you consider the negative amortization of a reverse mortgage. But there will likely be more money and appreciation in the second bucket, and no taxes have to be paid when pulling money from bucket three. The experts agree that if you pull money from bucket three early in retirement, then the portfolio longevity of bucket two will, of course, go up, as will your overall net worth. It is obvious that you have *less equity but more cash.* There is less in bucket three and more in bucket two. I encourage my clients to ask their children which bucket they would rather have more assets in—the second or the third—and most choose the second bucket. Those assets are easier to quantify and ultimately, easier to distribute. For example, anyone who has ever tried to sell houses in an estate can relate to that. You have to pay utilities, taxes, and upkeep to take care of the place while dropping the price to find a quick buyer. It is almost always best to preserve bucket two with bucket three.

The bottom line is that those three buckets of milk from my farm were the same milk. It did not matter which one you sold to the dairy; all had the same value when you poured it out. This is a simple but difficult concept to understand. Most people don't realize that when you pull money from bucket two, you are losing not only the asset but also whatever gains you will make in the future with that investment. There are either real costs or opportunity costs, no matter which bucket you draw from. Many advisors and clients worry about compound interest working against them from the reverse mortgage in bucket three, but they forget about the compound interest working for them at a greater rate in bucket two. It is not free to pull money from bucket two—there is always either a tax cost or an opportunity cost.

When you use bucket three early in retirement, your income will be greater and your retirement nest egg will last longer. Was that not the plan from the beginning?

This story ended with a happily ever after. Isaac graduated from the University of Wisconsin–Madison with a degree in finance and real estate. One of the last papers he wrote was titled "Reverse Mortgages—No Longer the Loan of Last Resort: A True Retirement Tool." All four sons clearly understand the role of reverse mortgages in our retirement *and* their legacy. When they send me birthday cards, they know how many years we have until my wife and I can qualify for our own reverse mortgage as part of our happily ever after.

CHAPTER 6

SEX, DRUGS, AND REVERSE MORTGAGES

I understand what you're saying, and
your comments are valuable, but
I'm gonna ignore your advice
ROALD, DAHL—BRITISH NOVELIST, SHORT STORY
WRITER, POET, SCREENWRITER, AND FIGHTER PILOT.

This is quite a way to start a chapter! But what do the words in this chapter's title have in common? Are they all bad things? No. They are all things that are neither good nor bad by themselves. All of them can be very good, helpful things, and all of them can be very destructive, even deadly, things.

For example, a life-saving drug for your spouse is nothing like the drug addiction that could kill your teenager, yet both substances are drugs. Sex can be misused in today's society, yet we believe that God created it to be one of the most sacred and wonderful experiences that a committed couple can enjoy. But if you hear the average opinions about reverse mortgages, then you would assume they are all bad, evil, and something to be avoided if at all possible. In fact, according to the last NRMLA poll of retirees and pre-retirees, almost nine out of ten hope they never have to get an HECM. Many advisors and clients listen to our story and then ignore the advice (as in the quote by Roald Dahl that opens this chapter) and overwhelming facts on the side of using an HECM early and go back to what they did before, dictated by hearsay and conventional wisdom.

Remember that the fairy godmother used a pumpkin, some mice, and a girl in rags to deliver a beautiful wife to the prince? Things are not always as they seem.

The purpose of this book is to try to understand the psychology behind the resistance to and fear of using reverse mortgages. When people think something is bad, it is often impossible for them to see the good. They look only at the negative aspects of the product and not at the good it can do. They look only at what is lost instead of what is gained. It's basic human nature to concentrate on what we lose instead of what we gain. I have met so many people who say, "Oh, reverse mortgages. That's where you lose the house, or that's where you lose all that equity." Of course, when you do a reverse mortgage, you will spend some or all of your equity. If you go to the grocery store and spend $200 dollars on groceries, you don't walk out and think you lost $200 in the store. You know that you have *traded* $200 for food worth $200. You consider that a fair transaction. It is a trade and not a loss. It's no different when you get to retirement and you trade equity for cash or for long-term care insurance, a vacation, a grandson's college education, or for any number of other things to make the last quarter of your life more fun and profitable. You have not lost anything; you have simply *traded home equity for something more valuable.*

If reverse mortgages are properly used, then they can and will save the retirements of millions of baby boomers. They are not to be used to take out lump sums to put into dubious investments or the casino. Does that sometimes happen? Of course. Any product can be misused. Some people have wasted their IRAs or their savings accounts. I have heard many people say, "Those reverse mortgages are awful. My uncle died, and there was nothing left in his house—the bank took it all. There was no equity left for the children." But I never heard anyone say, "My uncle died in his nineties, and his IRA was empty. Those dang IRAs—nobody should get them because, at the end, there's nothing left!" We have to be careful with our resources in retirement, no matter where they come from. Everyone has a limited amount, regardless of how much they have. You must prudently manage your spending buckets to leave a legacy for the next generation.

The idea that people who take out reverse mortgages become wasteful and spendthrifts is simply not true. In doing these mortgages since 2003, most of my clients have become more cautious with the home equity that we gave them and spend it more carefully than even their IRAs or their savings accounts. Money is a two-edged sword and can be used either prudently or foolishly. It can be used for good or bad. In the hands of a prudent retiree helped by a good financial advisor, a reverse mortgage is a good and valuable tool to create a better and safer retirement. Then we all live happily ever after!

But what about the government—doesn't this hurt the taxpayer?

It is rather ironic that the same people who feel this is a bad idea for seniors also feel this is a bad idea for taxpayers. It can't be both! If the government is paying out and creating big losses in the mortgage insurance program at FHA, then that means the borrowers are getting the long end of the stick. The truth is that any insurance program needs to be consistently reviewed to make sure the cost of premiums collected and assets guaranteed are in equilibrium. While I was writing this book, there was a pretty big political change in Washington, and we received a new HUD secretary who oversees FHA and the HECM program.

Dr. Ben Carson, the new secretary, talked about the HECM program in his remarks at LeadingAge Florida's annual convention in ChampionsGate, Florida, on July 17, 2017: "This is a top priority for my department: To give seniors more opportunities, more alternatives, more choices, and, if desired, to help more people age in place."

Carson called financial health one of "three essential initiatives for our nation's seniors."

"As reverse mortgages have become more popular, we have learned more about the needs of seniors," Carson continued.

He gave a detailed history of the program, acknowledging previous issues with the product such as imprudent draw amounts and the lack of nonborrowing spouse protections.

"These problems have lingered and need to be addressed. Adjustments needed to be made...The Founding Fathers wanted you and me to determine our needs and our spending, not some far-off monarchy in Europe or some self-interest in Washington," Carson said. "And our freedom is a continuous struggle. Every day we fight for freedom, looking for ways to have more choices, to make up our own minds, and to use our resources for our needs, in our own way.

"Housing counseling (for reverse mortgages) helps people buy a home and helps many people stay in their homes," Carson said. "They will be able to age in place. There will be more financial freedom, more responsible practices, and greater security for seniors.

Carson said in a tweet on August 29, 2017: "We're taking needed and prudent steps to put the HECM program on a more sustainable footing."

Several changes were then implemented in the program, starting with all applications taken after October 2, 2017. Changes will continue to take place in the program to ensure that all parties involved live happily ever after.

CHAPTER 7

WHAT ABOUT THE STEPSISTERS?

Parents, the children will be fine.
Spend their inheritance now.
—RON LIEBER

One easily forgotten part of the Cinderella story (which varies in some versions) is how things ended up for the mean stepsisters. In the nicer version, they moved to the palace with Cinderella and married some lesser lords in the kingdom. Regardless, they didn't have to worry about having a home to live in. I'm also sure that after Cinderella moved to the palace, she had no interest in moving back home after her parents passed away.

That brings up the most fascinating, strange, and crazy thought process that continues to amaze me as seniors think about their children, inheritances, and the house.

Stand outside that grocery store and ask all the pre-retirees and retirees what they want for their homes after they pass away. About 99 percent will tell you they would like to pass on their homes to their children free and clear. That's amazing because statistics show that only about 1 percent of children move into their parents' houses when they pass away. Sometimes I ask parents to picture this: "It's your funeral, and you're the last spouse to pass away. Your children all come to your funeral with big U-Haul trucks full of their furniture and dishes and the grandchildren still at home in tow. After the sorrowful tears at the gravesite, all the children, spouses, and grandkids drive to your house and start moving in." Is that the way it works? It is highly unlikely that your kids will move into your house. Let me say it again: it is highly unlikely that your kids will move into your house. Ninety-nine percent of the time, they drive to the Realtor's office, put the house up for sale, and take one of the first offers that comes in so they don't have to pay taxes and utilities or maintain the home.

So 99 percent of parents want to give their houses to their kids, and 99 percent of kids want to sell them as soon as they can. Now that is silly, but the vast majority of seniors never think through this.

It's not the house that you want to pass on, and it's not the house your kids are interested in inheriting—it's the *value* of the house. Don't forget how important that principle is.

Let's look at this more closely. When you pass away, you will likely be in your eighties or nineties, and your children will be in their fifties and sixties. If they don't have houses by now, then that may be a problem all by itself. In fact, some of them will be ready to retire and to get reverse mortgages themselves! In the discussion of inheritances in a previous chapter, we came to the conclusion that the longer you live, the smaller the inheritance for your children. The best way to give them the most amount of money is to die as soon as you retire! I would argue that if your kids would want you to die early so they can get your money, then you should disinherit them right now. However, if you wish to leave a legacy or to provide a home for your children, then what are you waiting for? It would be better if they inherited their own homes as compared to your home. Most people don't have enough money to buy homes for their children, but if they took money out of their houses or out of their investments, then they would be able to help their children while they're alive, perhaps with a down payment. They could give with a warm hand instead of a cold hand. Where did the idea come from that an inheritance should be given only after you're dead? It makes sense to give your heirs some of your money now while you can give your wealth away with your wisdom. You should first take care of your own financial needs, long-term care plans, insurances, and so on. But once you know you have enough for yourself, there's nothing wrong with giving while you're alive. Maybe you could take vacations with your children or grandchildren, help pay for college expenses, help with business investments or real estate, or whatever would seem to make sense in passing on wealth and wisdom to your family.

The emotions and ideas surrounding this topic are fascinating and controversial. To get an idea of how people think about this, see Ron Lieber's 2014 article in the *New York Times*, "Parents, the Children Will Be Fine. Spend Their Inheritance Now." The article is excellent and discusses reverse mortgages as the central theme. He ended the article by saying to his parents: *"Spend what you have and have faith that the education and life skills you already gave me are more than enough. I don't want an inheritance, nor do I expect one."* What is really interesting were the hundreds of comments that followed the article. There was a firestorm of very entitled potential heirs who are not only depending on that money but also expecting it.

What Is Your Legacy?

That brings up another important point. Is it your responsibility to leave behind a legacy of money? You may want to leave behind a life insurance policy, some stocks and bonds, or maybe even some gold coins. But I would argue that leaving behind well-adjusted children who are good husbands, wives, parents, employees, and community members who you helped shape with good values, love, and kindness is far more important than any monetary asset. I'm not advocating wasting your home equity for no good reason, but saving it and giving it to your children for no good reason doesn't make sense either. While we would like to leave a legacy behind for our four sons, we would not consider ourselves failures if I left them nothing monetarily. Whatever help we can give them while we are alive, in addition to encouraging them to be loving, contributing members of society to make this world a better place, is my biggest and most important goal. Maybe a family vacation today would be better than money spent on a big funeral meal?

Another responsibility that you have is to ensure that things are put in order and that everyone is aware of your wishes after you pass from this earth. So many people are in denial that the day will come when they will not be here to explain how they would like things divided up and how all their final affairs should be handled. The vast majority of people I've worked with over the age of sixty-two have not completed in writing their final wishes and directions. There's really no excuse for that because usually retired people have more time and money to be able to accomplish this task. Sometimes it involves an attorney, and I encourage clients who take out reverse mortgages to use some of the proceeds to pay for an attorney to complete an estate plan. You must start somewhere. The following website can help: www.theconversationproject.org.

Let's consider the fact that, at the end, both buckets two and three—retirement nest egg and home equity—could all be gone if we live long enough. And isn't that OK? We worked hard and then we played hard in retirement and left a legacy for the next generation in wisdom, even if there was very little money left. Quite frankly, when I received my inheritance from my parents, I felt sad. I wished Mom and Dad would've spent more of their money on going out to eat or on vacation or on simply enjoying their retirement. While I appreciated what I received, I think they deserved to spend more of it on themselves. They had already left a huge inheritance of wisdom, values, and memories that could not be denominated into dollars and cents. What they gave us besides the money was priceless.

In 2016, Barry Sacks, a tax attorney from California, along with some colleagues, published an article in the *Journal of*

Taxation that is a big bright spot for children of parents who have a reverse mortgage.

The gist of the article explains that it is possible for your children to deduct some or all of the unpaid interest and mortgage insurance that has not been paid by you while you lived in the home. While the children may be receiving taxable inheritances such as an IRA, or simply have a lot of income themselves, the HECM interest could potentially erase tens of thousands of dollars in required taxes that the children will not have to pay. Even if there is no equity left, then a very large tax deduction may help your children years from now after you are gone.

I'll end this chapter with a funny but sad story. There's one thing the reverse mortgage will not allow you to ever leave as an inheritance to your children. That is a debt. So many parents worry about living too long and the house not going up in value and that dreaded line crossing where more is owed on the house than it is worth. If that happens, then you can be sure the FHA will cover the excess amount owed, and neither your children nor you or your estate will owe the difference. It is possible for all the equity to be used up in your home, as we have discussed before. But this is a loan that is owed by the house and not by a person. If the house does not have enough equity to pay off the loan, then you or your children do not owe the difference. Instead, the lender will make a claim to the FHA mortgage insurance premium (MIP) fund after the house is sold. If your children wish to get the house back, then they can pay the mortgage balance *or* 95 percent of the appraised value—whichever is lower.

A few years ago, I was asked by a potential client to come to his house with an application because he was ready to do a loan. That's a little unusual because most people don't ask to complete an application before we have even met. But I followed his instructions, printed off an application, and drove to his house. The first indication I had that he was not the friendliest person in the world was when I got lost and stopped to ask a neighbor for directions. The neighbor said, "Oh, so you have an appointment with him? Good luck!" That made me a little nervous, but I continued down the dirt road to the potential client's home.

He was gruff and short, but he invited me into his home and gave me a place to set up on his kitchen counter. I asked if his wife was also available. "No," he said. "I divorced her a long time ago." Then he asked, "Do you have the application for the reverse mortgage?" I said I did. "Before I start signing, I have only one question. If I borrow the maximum amount and live a long time, then is it possible for me to leave a great big debt behind for my children?" I explained that he could use all his equity—but no more—and if there was money left, then his children would inherit the difference. He said, "But what if I owe more than the house is worth? Wouldn't they then have to come up with the difference?"

"No," I said. "That's why this is an FHA-insured loan. Your children can never owe more than what the house is worth."

"Then pack up your bags and leave," he told me. I was shocked. He had read some things on the Internet and was sure it was possible to leave behind a big debt for his children. He said, "I'm estranged from all four of my children. I don't like any of them, and they don't like me. I wanted to leave a big mess behind for them, but since you can't help me, you can leave."

He is the only person I've run into in my entire career who wanted to hurt his children and leave a big debt behind for them. I was happy to pack my bags and leave! I could see why he was alone at the end of his life. One of the overwhelmingly positive things about reverse mortgages is that they usually are not only a help to the clients but also to their children. You can't hurt them even if you try! The bumper sticker you see on all those motor homes that says "I'm spending our children's inheritance" doesn't really apply to reverse mortgages. As you spend bucket three, you are saving bucket two for them. The idea that a reverse mortgage is bad for the kids is a myth that was repeated so many times that some people started to believe it.

The truth is that they too can live happily ever after—because you got the reverse mortgage and enjoyed your life and then passed on to them any remaining equity and a tax deduction as icing on the cake.

CHAPTER 8

THE COSTS-EXPENSIVE GLASS SLIPPERS

It's unwise to pay too much, but it's worse to pay too little. When you pay too much, you lose a little money—that's all. When you pay too little, you sometimes lose everything, because the thing you bought was incapable of doing the thing it was bought to do. The common law of business balance prohibits paying a little and getting a lot—it can't be done.

—John Ruskin

The fairy godmother did not skimp on the clothes, jewelry, and carriage. She knew she needed to give the best presentation possible if Cinderella was going to get into the ball.

Even glass slippers can be expensive. I noticed that prices range from $4.99 on Etsy for a pair of acrylic glass slippers to a single Swarovski crystal slipper for ninety-nine dollars. Both are very different for different purposes.

Price has been the topic of products since the first salespeople went from one village to the next a few thousand years ago. The price being too high is simply an opinion based on what value you can get from the product. Is one pill worth $1,000? We all would gladly pay $1,000 for that pill if it would save our lives, but if it would only eliminate our headaches, then we likely would not pay even one dollar for it.

Those of us who work with reverse mortgages every day believe they are inexpensive for what they guarantee. Typically, you will give up between 3 and 4 percent of the value of your home in the form of equity—not cash— to pay for the closing costs associated with a reverse mortgage. The biggest cost is typically the FHA MIP. Most mortgage insurance only protects the lender. The MIP for reverse mortgages not only protects the lender but also protects you and your children from ever owing more than what the house is worth. It also guarantees that you can live in your house for the rest of your life—no matter what—by paying only taxes and insurance. If you give up just a very small portion of your equity in exchange for these guarantees, then that is an excellent trade.

In chapter 4, we compared a HELOC to a HECM LOC. You know that HELOCs cost very little or nothing at all, but if you're eighty-five and lose your line of credit after your husband has passed, then you now owe $150,000 without the ability to pay it back. That inexpensive HELOC could turn out to be the most expensive loan with the worst outcome of all.

Think about it: Do you always buy the cheapest thing you can get? Do you plan on trading in your car for a bike or a horse because they are cheaper? Do you start looking around for the cheapest heart surgeon when your husband needs surgery? When you go on a cruise, do you look for the ship that doesn't have all those expensive lifeboats to save a couple of bucks? I know that may seem silly, but it is true that we always weigh the value of what we're getting against the price we are paying. Cheapest is rarely the best option.

Why don't you try this? Walk into a bank that does not offer reverse mortgages. Tell the banker you would like a loan for about half the value of your home at a relatively low interest rate that you will only make payments on when you want to, and if you don't want to, then the payment won't be due until a year after you and your spouse have both died or decided to move. And one more thing—if the housing market crashes and you live to be 105, your kids will give the bank all the proceeds from the sale of the house, but they won't have to pay the difference. What do you think the banker will tell you? He or she would either laugh at you or refer you to a lender that does HECM reverse mortgages.

Let's put this into perspective. A HECM is a loan you pay back after you die or when you no longer need it or want it. Then you are released from a personal guarantee, and you are guaranteed to live in your home—no matter what—for the rest of your life with no payments, regardless of interest rates, home values, overall market conditions, or economy forecasts.

The cost for that privilege only averages 3 to 4 percent of your home value, but you don't pay for that in cash—you pay in the form of giving up some of your equity. If you live long enough or your home value drops, then you may never pay your closing costs or even all the accrued interest.

If your house goes up by 5 percent the next year or over the next few years, then the HECM costs you nothing, as it was paid for by the equity increase. If it goes down, then you are lucky you took out the cash before the drop. You don't lose sleep over your house going up or down by 5 percent because you know you are there for the long run. So giving up less than 5 percent of equity is really not a big deal because you are not paying it—the house is!

Will You Ever Pay It?

The program is set up assuming the value of your home will go up in value over the years you have the HECM. That increase in value is expected to not only cover the initial closing costs but also the ongoing interest. But, we know that doesn't always happen—what happens then? When my uncle passed away, his house owed about $20,000 more than what it was worth. I remember him being concerned about the $6,000 worth of closing costs fourteen years before when he took out the loan. He also worried about the interest costs every time he looked at his monthly statements. His house with the beautiful green sinks and red shag carpet did not go up in value like updated houses in bigger cities. But neither he nor his heirs paid for the closing costs or the thousands of dollars worth of interest. The equity in the house that he used to enjoy his last years was put to good use, and there were other assets his heirs received, but they were not liable to pay back the shortfall—it was paid for by the FHA mortgage insurance.

Different Currency: Everything Has a Cost

It's important to know that we are paying for the reverse mortgage closing costs and interest in a different currency. It is the currency of home equity—not cash from bucket one or bucket two.

Any money used in retirement has a cost associated with it. To get money out of bucket one, you have to go to work to trade your time for money. To make an extra thousand or two in retirement, you may have to work twenty hours every week. If you take money out of bucket two, then there are costs associated with all the investments. There are management fees and commissions and insurance costs. There are also opportunity costs. If you take money out of bucket two, then you're not only taking out $10,000 but also everything that investment will earn for the next ten, twenty, or thirty years of retirement. Many people think that the compound interest is so very expensive in reverse mortgages, but if you pull money out of a reverse mortgage instead of taking it from bucket two, then that means the miracle of compound interest will work for you in bucket two more than it will work against you in bucket three.

There are costs even if you sell your home. Those typical fees would be 6 to 8 percent, including moving costs, which then would need to be paid in cash.

Even if you don't pull money out of bucket three by getting a reverse mortgage, then you are still paying the costs in other areas without the privilege of having the cash flow.

In the words of Wade Pfau from his article in *Investment News*, "How reverse mortgages work as a source of retirement income" (October 16, 2016): "Generally, if one thinks about the investment portfolio and home equity as assets, then meeting spending goals requires spending from assets somewhere on the household balance sheet. In this regard, *spending from home equity should not be viewed as accumulating debt any more than spending from investment assets should be.* A reverse mortgage creates liquidity for an otherwise illiquid asset."

If you continue to make payments of, say, $2,000 per month, then that is $24,000 per year and $720,000— almost 3/4 of a million over thirty years. If closing costs are $5,000, $10,000, or even $25,000, then is that really a comparison?

What about Taxes?

One day, I went to see a client, parked in his driveway, and walked into his house through his open garage door. When I got inside, he asked me, "Did you see my fifty-thousand-dollar car in the garage?"

"No." I said. "I saw only a Chevy Impala."

He said, "That's the one!" I asked him why he paid so much for a car that should be worth only $30,000 or $35,000. He said, "That's why you're here. In December, I bought that nice black Chevrolet Impala for my wife as a Christmas present and wrapped it up with the big red bow, just like you see on TV. Later in April, my financial planner and tax advisor found out that I had taken that money from my IRA. It pushed me up into the next higher tax bracket, and because I didn't have money in other accounts, I had to pull more money out of my IRA, triggering more taxes. Just that one car purchase cost me almost twenty thousand dollars in taxes. My financial planner told me to call you."

The closing costs for his loan were less than ten thousand dollars. If he had used a reverse mortgage to buy the car in the first place, then he would not have lost all that money in taxes that cannot be recovered. So many people today have a significant amount of money in IRAs and other taxable retirement accounts. If they are not careful, then they will lose as much as one third of those accounts to the IRS. As we discussed previously, because reverse mortgage money is borrowed money, there is no taxation.

But It's Easy for Me to Make That Mortgage Payment

You've read this far, so you know that it really doesn't make sense to pay cash from buckets one or two to create equity in bucket three in retirement when you don't have to. However, millions of people make mortgage payments after they turn sixty-two, even though they don't have to. I had many people tell me it's only X dollars, and they can afford it. Just because we can afford something doesn't mean it makes sense to pay it. Maybe you can afford to buy a Ferrari, but that doesn't mean it would be a smart thing to do with your money.

There are more than sixty thousand people a month turning sixty-two and still making mortgage payments. Some of them can afford it for now. But most of them, if they lived into their eighties and nineties, will not be comfortable making those payments. Wade Pfau's research that is detailed in chapter 7 of his 2016 book illustrates the danger of making a mortgage payment when you don't have to. As mentioned before, the senior whom a reverse mortgage can most likely help is someone over sixty-two, with 50 percent equity or more, and still making a mortgage payment. Remember, it is not only $1,000 dollars per month but also $12,000 per year and $120,000 over ten years. If it's a thirty-year mortgage, then the cost is $360,000. While you will have more equity when you are in your nineties, you will have far less cash in bucket two. In fact, it will be hundreds of thousands of dollars less. Equity is not free. It has a huge cost in the form of cash. In retirement, cash is much more valuable than equity. It is surprising that people put such a high value on something that is so unusable.

It is very common for people to say, "I'm doing fine. I don't need a reverse mortgage—yet. Maybe I'll want one in the future, but for now, I'm enjoying paying off my house." They should ask themselves what the purpose is of the equity they are creating.

I would ask them to think about how much money they are losing by

- not taking out an HECM and using money from bucket two when they could let it grow;
- not getting tax savings for themselves or their heirs by strategically using the interest deductions;
- keeping money in a 0.00 percent (point nothing) savings account so they have ready cash available when they could use their credit line for the just-in-case money;
- pulling money from social security when they could wait a year or two or more and get a much bigger check;
- pulling money from stocks and bonds when they have dropped in price during market corrections;
- not having cash to keep a life insurance policy going; and
- not enjoying time with children and grandchildren, going on vacation, and all the fun things in life that they cannot put a monetary value on.

You see, it's all about opportunity cost, which is a much bigger issue than a small amount of equity that you are giving up. Remember, most people concentrate on the cost—not the benefit—when what they are losing versus what they are gaining is that much greater.

If you don't pay closing costs, interest, and MIP, then you will save a dime but lose a dollar.

The Real Cost: The Memories Factor

When it comes to cost, I think this is the biggest issue. I am going to tell you that you WILL give EVERYTHING away — someday— either with a cold hand or a warm hand! There were some pharaohs a few thousand years ago who thought they could take their stuff with them. As it turns out, all their stuff is still in the pyramids on this side of the river Styx! My father said there are no U-Hauls behind a hearse. Why, then, are there so many baby boomers storing $6 trillion in their homes when it could be used for all kinds of fun things with their children and grandchildren today? We all have seen the MasterCard commercials that end with a special experience that was "priceless." We have the opportunity as baby boomer retirees to turn some of our equity into cash that can create wonderful memories, helping those who are less fortunate than us, especially those in our own families. Storing thousands and thousands of dollars in our homes and eventually giving it away with a cold hand or losing it to health care really doesn't make a lot of sense. But the vast majority of baby boomers are doing just that because they have an irrational fear of the HECM reverse mortgage product and the costs that seem to be too expensive. The memories we leave behind are far more valuable than the home equity we are trying to store.

CHAPTER 9

THE BEAR IN THE CLOSET

F-E-A-R is an abbreviation for: False Evidence Appearing Real.
—ZIG ZIGLAR

Most people would have been scared of the mice that Cinderella had to bring to the fairy godmother so that she could turn them into horses to pull the carriage. But Cinderella obviously overcame that fear and thus had the transportation to get to the ball.

Fear and greed, we are told by psychologists, are two of the greatest motivators for any human being. It seems that fear is greater than greed in most situations. Despite the fact that a reverse mortgage line of credit can double, triple, maybe even, quadruple during someone's lifetime, potentially giving him or her more money than what the house is even worth, does not appear to encourage getting a loan motivated by greed. But there are many people who would be afraid to get a reverse mortgage, even if the closing costs were zero.

I remember when my in-laws decided to get a reverse mortgage to purchase their final retirement home. My father-in-law went down to the local coffee hangout and told his buddies what he was doing. Immediately, one of the ringleaders of the group said, "Albert, are you crazy? Don't you know that you will end up owing more on the house than it is worth, and after you die, your wife, Frannie, will be kicked out on the street and have no place to live? Who the hell is taking advantage of you?" After he told them it was his son-in-law, I knew I had some work to do! The fact is that none of these things was true, but by saying them, they created some fear, and if my in-laws weren't my close relatives, then this likely would have stopped them from getting a reverse mortgage, and they would have paid cash or taken out a traditional forward mortgage.

It is easy to be afraid of something that isn't really there. I experienced this personally when I was a little boy at home on the farm in Wisconsin. My bedroom was close to my parents' room in the old farmhouse, and if my dad was sleeping before me and he started to snore, then I was sure there was a bear in my closet. I would cry and run to my mother, and she would put her arms around me and take me to the closet, turn on the light, and prove to me that it was my father snoring and that there was no bear in the closet. I won't tell you how old I was until I stopped worrying about the bear in the closet, but I can tell you it was just as real in my mind as if one was actually in there.

In my current position, I usually do about three hundred speaking events per year to senior homeowners, real estate agents, financial advisors, and other professionals. Most of those events are nothing more than taking people to the reverse mortgage closet, turning on the lights, and eliminating the fear surrounding the HECM. Some people are more open-minded than others, but there are always several who are just too afraid of this safe, government-insured mortgage and try to do retirement without it.

It's Too Good to Be True

Some people tell me that the benefits of reverse mortgages are too good to be true. One of the advisors I work with in North Carolina said it's not too good to be true, BUT **it is too good to be free.** There is a cost, and you have to give up some of your equity to make this work. Because the FHA insures this, it is not too good to be true any more than a car insurance policy or life insurance, which pays out if you have a car crash or an untimely death. You have paid the premiums, and you are entitled to a claim if something goes wrong. The whole purpose of this program is to help people age in place. It is better for seniors and their children and for the government (and for the banks that offer reverse mortgages) for seniors to live in their homes for as long as they can.

This Is Not My Last Home

Another fear some people have is that they might have to move and that this might not be their last home. No one really knows if they are going to be in the house they currently are in for the rest of their lives. Kids move, health declines, the neighborhood changes—you may want to move or have to move. You are still protected by the same FHA insurance that your heirs are protected with. You get all the equity that is not used, and if you are upside down, then you are not required to pay it. Many people take out forward thirty-year mortgages and don't stay in those houses for thirty years. Some clients I have worked with are on their third or fourth reverse mortgages. Some have refinanced when home values went up, and others simply followed their children around the country. There are always costs in refinancing, but that is simply the cost of moving. Of course, you should not use a reverse mortgage for a year or two because there is no refund on the closing costs if you move to a different home, but you don't need to be in the house until you are 100 for it to make sense either. When you got married, you probably said, "Till death do us part." As the lender, we have to say that same pledge when you take the reverse mortgage, but as the borrower, you can pay it off any time you like without a penalty. If your home value goes up, then it costs very little to refinance and to get more money out if the numbers make sense. The cost on a refinance is very little and is sometimes completely free because of the insurance credit from when you first did your loan. The bottom line is that if you will be in your house for three to five years, then you should look into the possibility of an HECM.

Interest Rates and Arms

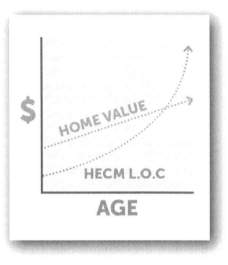

Adjustable interest rates are a big fear because usually the adjustable rate HECM LOC makes the most sense for clients looking to get the most money, even if they are drawing a big portion of the line right away. Fixed rates are also available but don't allow you to make payments and then get the money back out. You lose a lot of flexibility. In a regular mortgage, interest rates are always a concern because if an adjustable rate goes up, then your payment also goes up. But with a reverse mortgage, the payment is always zero. Yes, you will lose more equity if interest rates increase, but when interest rates go up, so does your line of credit, potential tax deductions, and monthly payments paid to you. If rates start skyrocketing—which is unlikely—then you will see a big increase in your available line of credit. All interest rates are capped at either 5 or 10 percent from the start rate, and an HECM interest rate usually runs only about a half or one percent higher than a regular forward mortgage. As you delve further into the HECM product, you will soon see that the interest rates and closing costs are not nearly as important as they are in traditional forward mortgages. They simply operate differently, and your loss of equity is always capped by the home's value. If interest rates skyrocket, then that could be a very good thing for you because you will receive more money in your line of credit, and potentially, a higher tax deduction. If the rates go too high and they exceed the value of the home, then you will not be required to make the payment. The FHA mortgage insurance is there for that exact reason. With a regular mortgage, you might be forced out of the house because you can't make the payment. With a reverse mortgage, the FHA guarantees that not only can you can stay in your home, even if the value of your home is exceeded by the mortgage—by a lot or a little— BUT you also may receive more money in your line of credit AND potentially a higher tax deduction as well. With a forward mortgage, lower rates are always better, but with a reverse, often higher interest rates are better! They call that counterintuitive.

Not Knowing

The vast majority of fears—the bank will take the house, I will have to move when my husband dies, my children will get a big bill after our funeral, we will never be able to move, the government will tell me what to do, and more—are simply untrue. But the worst fear of all is a simple one. Seniors say, "I heard they were bad, and we are simply going to stay away." It's not really the expensive costs, compound interest, fear of the lender, or even concern for the kids; it is simply the fear that there must be something in the dark that's going to get them someday—very similar to the bear in my closet. It is wise to be afraid of a real bear in the closet. It is unwise to lose sleep over an empty closet that has no bears in it. I am sure Cinderella would've felt awful if she had not had the courage to pick up the mice who turned out to be strong horses to get her to her destination. The FHA HECM reverse mortgage is a powerful force that can give you a better and safer retirement and your family a better inheritance. Being afraid to use it without a good reason is likely a very big mistake.

The next chapter is about the fairy godmother, which should take away a majority of the fear surrounding reverse mortgages.

CHAPTER 10

HUD-THE FAIRY GODMOTHER

*Why couldn't life come with guarantees? Or
while I was at it, how about a Fairy Godmother
to make all my dreams come true?*
—STACIE SIMPSON, ROMANCE AUTHOR

Let's face it: without the fairy godmother, Cinderella would never have had a dance with the prince!

The promises that come with a reverse mortgage would not be possible without the FHA Federal Housing Administration, which is part of HUD, Housing and Urban Development. If the FHA mortgage insurance was not involved with this loan, then I would not be writing this book. I would not have been involved with more than one thousand of these loans, including for friends and family, and I would not be planning to get one the day my wife and I turn sixty-two in a few short years.

The second chapter of Shelley Giordano's book, *What's the Deal with Reverse Mortgages?* (2015), does a great job of telling the history of how the FHA brought this product to where it is today. The home equity conversion mortgage referred to in this book as the HECM started during President Reagan's term in the 1980s as a pilot program and now is available to anyone over sixty-two who meets the program's qualifications. There have been major changes since the crash in 2008 that makes the program better, safer, and more able to survive for the long term.

Personally, I am not a big fan of government programs, but this program is an example of a public and private partnership that works. Government money does not fund these loans. There is an insurance fund—the FHA MIP fund—that insures and guarantees the loans that are done by private mortgage companies and banks. Some people think this is a taxpayer-funded program, but that is not the case. Many baby boomers bought their first houses with an FHA loan with a small down payment that is covered by the same insurance fund that covers the losses in the reverse mortgage program. The insurance fund is designed to be revenue neutral for the government because the insurance premiums paid by borrowers fund the losses over a large number of loans, just like homeowners or any other type of insurance. That is why these loans have more expensive closing costs. The insurance is what makes the wheels go around for everyone.

There have been several private reverse mortgages done over the years on both a small and a large scale. Many of those have failed and have given the whole industry a bad name. Some of them required borrowers to share leftover equity. Others were nothing more than balloon loans that often came due before the borrower passed away. The HECM is a safe, FHA-insured loan. As the industry grows, there may be more proprietary private products. There are already a few jumbo products available in a few states. It is inevitable that other good products will eventually come from the private sector. However, currently, more than 95 percent of reverse mortgages are HECMs. For the time being, that is the safest route until the industry has done a lot more than one million loans that have been closed since the 1980s. As I mentioned in chapter 2, we are in uncharted waters. The program is in partnership with HUD and NRMLA in underwriting, qualifications, and actuarial calculations. At this writing, there have been some projected losses, (not real losses) so we know that is what prompted the Oct, 2nd, 2017 changes that Ben Carson talked about in the summer of 2017. We covered some of that in chapter 6. So because of the economic perils of the program, sometimes people ask, "Is this going to be around in the future?" No one really knows the answer to that, but the strong opinion of those of us in the industry for more than a decade is that it most certainly will be around—simply not in the current form. Every year there is an actuarial report that tries to predict life expectancies, interest rates, draw rates, home values and many other hard to predict factors. Because of wide swings and differing opinions of the future, the only thing constant about the HECM program is change. Quite frankly, that is another reason you should take advantage of the program if you are "of age". Don't argue with the Fairy Godmother with a wand! A bird in the hand.....

But here is the real reason we think it will be around for the baby boomers for a long time. When I was a kid, my mom would ask me, "Harlan, what if everyone was like you in school, or at the Cub Scout meeting, or in church—what would those groups be like?" So when I started in this industry, I asked myself mom's question. What if everyone over sixty-two got a reverse mortgage? When the actuarial numbers are properly calculated, the more people who participate in any insurance program helps spread the risk over more people. When more people pay insurance premiums, there is a greater chance of success. Believe me, with 50 percent of the federal budget being put toward social security, Medicare, and Medicaid, this will continue to be a need in the future.

As I mentioned before, my strong recommendation to anyone over sixty-two is to not wait. Take advantage of the opportunity that is here now. These loans are non-recourse. That means your loan can never change once you close unless you decide to pay it off early. Future loans may be different and harder to qualify for. I didn't really understand it, but my father said on many occasions on our farm back in Wisconsin, "Don't look a gift horse in the mouth. Appreciate what you're given." If the fairy godmother turns a pumpkin into a coach, then I would just jump in it and head for the castle. The FHA HECM is a great carriage to get you where you want to go in retirement.

CHAPTER 11

HORSELESS CARRIAGES, ELECTRICITY, AND TELEPHONES

*This "telephone" has too many shortcomings to be
seriously considered as a means of communication.
The device is inherently of no value to us.*
—WESTERN UNION INTERNAL MEMO, 1876

The facts are clear: Cinderella was a better choice for the prince's future than any of the mean (some versions say ugly) stepsisters.

The facts are also clear that tapping home equity early in retirement with HECM reverse mortgages is a better choice than ignoring home equity or using it only as a last resort. The research and facts compiled by many smart people in the financial-planning world are overwhelming. It is likely that the $6 trillion in home equity—and growing every day— is a major part of the solution to the retirement income crisis we are facing for the next couple of decades.

But remember the Wikipedia (2017) definition of Cinderella from our first chapter: "The word 'Cinderella' has, by analogy, come to mean *one whose attributes were unrecognized, or one who unexpectedly achieves recognition or success after a period of obscurity and neglect.*"

When will HECMs come out of the shadows of "obscurity and neglect" and become recognized and successful at changing the way retirement is done in this country?

When will the wedding happen between proactive financial planning and baby boomer seniors?

It will take a tipping point like Malcolm Gladwell (2000) described in his book of the same name: "The tipping point is that magic moment when an idea, trend, or social behavior crosses a threshold, tips, and spreads like wildfire. Just as a single sick person can start an epidemic of the flu, so too can a small but precisely targeted push cause a fashion trend or the popularity of a new product."

For years, the reverse mortgage industry has served only about fifty thousand people each year, even though millions more are eligible. Why is this the case? No one really knows for sure, but this book was written to investigate this question and to be part of the solution. At a dinner meeting, a colleague told me that we simply "cannot change the hearts and minds of America's seniors." I simply disagree. Baby boomers are an incredibly smart group of people who have dramatically shaped our world in many ways—they are not just a bunch of lemmings following one another over the proverbial cliff. If we give them the right information in the right way, then they will collectively change the way retirement is done in this country.

I believe there are four things that need to happen.

The Reverse Mortgage Industry Must Change the Message

We have met the enemy, and it is us.

A client who recently closed on his own reverse mortgage wrote this on his comment sheet: "At our age and stage in life, one doesn't wish to be in a situation financially of asking for financial assistance and in need of money to live."

That's our fault—that's how we branded the product!

As an industry, newspaper ads, direct mail pieces, and heavy television advertising with older actors have branded this product as a loan of last resort so people like this client think they have failed. It's like the billboard I saw for a personal injury attorney. It read: "In a wreck? Get a check. Call us today." We must change the perception that this is a loan of last resort—a mark of failure, a mark of giving up. You don't have to be old, broke, and stupid to get a reverse mortgage. This is not something you have to do because you planned wrong or because you made mistakes. *This should be part of your plan right from the beginning.* Just like you deposited money into an IRA, savings account, or annuity, you have also deposited money into a house account, which we've called bucket three. Taking money out of bucket three is no different from taking money out of any other asset. It is simply a planned and proper use of your assets and your overall net worth.

Some in our industry will continue to advertise this product as a loan of last resort. Quite frankly, those in desperate need will respond more quickly to advertising. So it will be advertised as an emergency funding tool for when you need to buy prescriptions or to pay for basic living. Certainly, we want to help people who are in those situations. But the smartest and best way is to properly use the home equity at the beginning of retirement so that choosing between medicine and food will never have to happen. Preventing an accident before it happens is always the best way to do things. You've heard the adage "an ounce of prevention is worth a pound of cure." If we don't do something now, then there will be too many retirement crashes five, ten, fifteen, and twenty years down the road.

We believe that advertising this product as a retirement planning tool, not as an ambulance, is going to be a big part of that tipping point.

Public Perception Must Change

This has happened before. No one really liked horseless carriages when they first came out; in fact, some cities tried to outlaw their use. Marcel Bich had problems selling pens when he came to this country from France—people said they already had plenty of pencils and didn't need more writing utensils. We know that eventually Bic ball point pens became the standard, and a few more pens than pencils and fountain pens are sold each year. Many people warned against wiring homes with electricity because of the potential for fires (not that gas lamps hadn't caused a few fires before). Imagine your home without electricity! The quote that opens this chapter showed that the telegraph company could not envision the telephone as a form of communication.

According to NRMLA, which monitors the media treatment of reverse mortgages, in 2016, for the first time, there were more than 90 percent positive or neutral articles in newspapers and magazines and on TV. But they also discovered that 86 percent of baby boomers are not interested in getting a reverse mortgage. We believe it is just a matter of time before public acceptance will be similar to media acceptance. Good news travels slowly, but it still travels.

The Government Must Promote What Helps the Budget

One of the biggest beneficiaries of this program is the entity that created it. Since the government, through the FHA, started the pilot program in the 1980s, it has been a help for seniors, which in turn is a help to the government. Yet neither political party nor any president has ever publicly spoken out about the positives of the HECM program. Most comments are negative or are about the need for increasing regulation. In reality, education is what's truly needed.

If we look at the overall view of how the government would be affected if there was widespread use of the reverse mortgage product, then it is very encouraging. As mentioned earlier, half of the government budget is social security, Medicaid, and Medicare. If just a small part of the $6 trillion dollars in senior equity was used for long-term-care costs alone, then it would go a long way toward alleviating the huge Medicaid problem. The next chapter will discuss the synergy between long-term care and reverse mortgages. My own parents were able to use the equity in their home for long-term care costs to keep them at home before they passed away. That alleviated the government paying out tens of thousands of dollars for a Medicaid nursing home. And wasn't that better for Mom and Dad as well?

Financial Advisors' Recommendations

Up until a few years ago, the financial-planning community completely ignored the reverse mortgage product. In fact, FINRA (Financial Industry Regulatory Authority) actually recommended against it in all cases and called it the "reversal of fortune." Then, starting with the first article in the *Journal of Financial Planning* in 2012, there was one research article after another proving the value of the reverse mortgage as a true retirement tool best used at age sixty-two, not at eighty-two or ninety-two. FINRA has changed the advisory on its website, as prompted by Barry Sacks, one of the researchers.

But still, 90 percent of the rank-and-file financial advisors are just like the 90 percent of seniors who think that a reverse mortgage is the loan of last resort. I had a financial advisor at a seminar in Atlanta raise his hand in the back of the room. He said, "I find it difficult to recommend the product that is sold next to Ginsu knives on late-night cable TV." It is important, actually critical, that financial advisors, attorneys, and CPAs drop their prejudices and preconceived ideas and read the articles and the research that their industry has published. There are many of us reverse mortgage professionals who don't advertise with the Ginsu knives!

In the spring of 2017, I was talking with John Salter, a professor at Texas Tech University, who has done a large amount of research about reverse mortgages and financial planning and who has authored several papers. He works with Harold Evensky as a financial advisor. He commented that sometimes he serves as an expert witness in lawsuits involving financial advisors. John projected into the future by wondering how he could possibly defend a financial advisor who did not tell his client about a safe, government-insured mortgage that could've increased the client's portfolio longevity or created cash availability in a HECM LOC so the client wouldn't run out of money. While there is risk in advertising the use of any financial product, there appears to be more risk in *not* talking about the benefits of an HECM reverse mortgage. Later in 2017, I worked with Jamie Hopkins, who is an attorney and an LLM, at a seminar in Denver, Colorado. He warned a room full of financial advisors that not talking about reverse mortgages is a legal risk that they should not take.

In presenting to hundreds a financial advisors over the years, I know that it is impossible for them to properly advise their clients on the use of a product they know very little or nothing about. But once they understand the value of the reverse mortgage in retirement planning, they can create a much safer, better, and longer-term retirement plan for their clients. If financial advisors do more than just talk about a reverse mortgage and instead use it as an overall tool in every plan rather than in just a few plans, then this will truly revolutionize the way that clients plan efficiently for retirement.

Wade Pfau refers to his plans as *efficient retirement income plans.* The definition of efficiency, in the way that he looks at it, is to get the maximum amount of income during the retiree's lifetime and still have the most left for a legacy at the end. In simple terms, make the most of what you have. When advisors look at a reverse mortgage as one more tool to create that efficiency, we will see the baby boomers making widespread use of their home equity.

As mentioned earlier in this book, Wade Pfau opened a December 2015 article in *Advisor Perspectives* with this quote: "Through inertia and stubbornness, old ideas die slowly. Financial advisors maintain a dismal view about reverse mortgages. However, much has changed in just the past few years. Revisit your outdated thinking with an open mind about a tool that is on the cusp of more widespread use."

And let's revisit another quote from chapter 1: "The lack of focus on home equity in retirement income planning is nothing short of a complete failure to properly plan and utilize all available retirement assets. This needs to change immediately because strategic uses of home equity, especially reverse mortgages, could save many people from financial failure in retirement and help stem the overall retirement income crisis facing Americans" (Hopkins 2015).

Baby boomers have a lot at stake and cannot afford to fail at retirement. There are no do-overs.

This reminds me of a sign in our home: "Enjoy Life Now—This Is Not a Rehearsal!"

Let's go to the last chapter so that we can retire happily ever after!

CHAPTER 12

HAPPILY EVER AFTER

*I'm more interested in the future than in the past,
because the future is where I intend to live.*

—ALBERT EINSTEIN

As with Cinderella, every fairy tale ends with three words: happily ever after. But we know that retirement not as simple as walking out the door on your last day on the job, going home, and putting your feet up and everything will be happy for the rest of your life. It's a lot more complicated than that. This book does not pretend to know all the answers either financially or psychologically for how the last quarter of your life should go. But, hopefully, we have given you some concrete ideas as to how to use an HECM in your personal situation.

Reading books heavy on theory sometimes irritates me. I like the author's ideas and concepts, but when I put down the book, I say, "What do I do now?" This last chapter will give you some very specific ideas and actions that others have taken once they understood the value and flexibility of a reverse mortgage.

If you are driving from Minneapolis to Dallas, there are many ways to get there. But there's only one way that is the most efficient. Reverse mortgages are all about getting from one end of your retirement to the other in the most efficient way. This chapter is not a substitute for reading Wade Pfau's book, *Reverse Mortgages: How to Use Reverse Mortgages to Secure Your Retirement* (2016), which is full of specific, well-researched, and detailed procedures. This chapter gives you the thirty-thousand-foot view, and his book goes to the street level. This book is also not designed or intended to give you specific financial, tax, or legal advice. That can be done only in a personal meeting with licensed, competent financial professionals. I work with several trained reverse mortgage professionals who team up with financial advisors nationwide who can give you a customized retirement plan based on your assets, plans, values, and goals using the principles of the research we have talked about in this book. That is where you should start after you get a taste of some of the options available to you as you read over these general applications. You should do business only with well-trained reverse mortgage loan officers who partner with attorneys, tax advisors, and financial planners, just like doctors who are specialists that merge their talents for the sake of a better patient outcome.

Here are the most common uses and recommendations that are made to clients inquiring about a reverse mortgage.

Eliminate an Existing Mortgage Payment
Some people think that you must have your house completely paid off before you can do a reverse mortgage.

That simply is not true. In fact, one of the most common uses of a reverse mortgage is to pay off an existing forward mortgage. If you are over sixty-two, have about 50 percent equity, and are still making a mortgage payment, then you could be one of the biggest beneficiaries of this program. Remember, if you have a $400,000 home, at sixty-two, you're eligible for about $160,000 in a reverse mortgage loan under the 2017 changes. (Check with your professional because your age and interest rate dramatically changes your available loan amount and it can change frequently.) Let's say that you have a $150,000 mortgage that you're still making $1,000 monthly payments on. (By the way, that is $12,000 per year and more than 200,000 dollars in fifteen years, and you will still be making payments for a couple of years after that. A reverse mortgage of $160,000 would pay off your existing loan and allow you never to make payments unless you wanted to for tax purposes. You would still have the $10,000 remaining in a HECM LOC to use for future needs. There are millions of people still continuing to make a mortgage payment, moving money from buckets one and two and trying to create more equity in bucket three. It really doesn't make sense, but that's what conventional wisdom and habit make people do. Talk to your financial advisor about what the effect of eliminating a mortgage payment will do to your overall plan. Housing is generally the largest expense in retirement. By eliminating the mortgage payment, you need only to pay taxes, insurance, and home owner association fees, which dramatically decreases your expenses.

Over sixty-two, more than 50 percent equity, still making a mortgage payment? *Stop it*—you don't need to!

Purchasing Your Retirement Home with a Reverse Mortgage HECM

There are lots of folks who think that a reverse mortgage is only for people who already own a home. But, there are many baby boomers— more than 700,000 every year who are buying a move-up or move-down home. We like to call that rightsizing and there is a growing group of real estate agents—many of them Senior Real Estate Specialists (SRES) who help seniors to sell their current home and buy the home they plan to keep for the duration of retirement. If you are not in the home you plan to be in for the foreseeable future- why don't you move now? Why wait until you are forced to move when you lose a spouse or get sick or have a stroke? There is more than enough stress at that time. I have always told my clients to not wait. If you need to move to a one story home, or have wider doorways or no steps— do it now. If you would like to retire on a golf course or a lake or nearer to your children— what are you waiting for? If you want the gourmet kitchen, the home theatre, the big front porch—you are not getting any younger— now is the time! So how does a reverse mortgage work on a purchase?

The first thing to be aware of is that a reverse mortgage requires you to have equity in a home and of course you have no equity in a home you are just purchasing so you will create the equity by putting a larger down payment than you would on a typical 20% down forward mortgage which requires payments for the next 15-30 years. That larger down payment will typically come from the sale of your current home and you will simply be transferring the equity from your old home to your new home to increase your buying power and to make sure you have no required payments except for taxes and insurance. Your downpayment will be between 60 and 65% if you are 62 or have a young spouse. If you are in your late 80's, you would only need about 30% down. Your down payment will always be calculated by the current interest rate and the age of the youngest borrower. The numbers below are only examples and you should talk to your lender to get exact numbers based on your personal situation.

Lets look at an example of downsizing first. Lets say you have sold your $500,000 big old 2 story in New England where you raised your children that has appreciated over the years and you still have a $160,000 mortgage remaining to pay off. The maintenance and taxes are quite expensive as well. You now decide to move by your children in the Carolina's where taxes and homes are a little less expensive. You find a nice home in a 55 + community for only $300,000 which has virtually no maintenance and cheaper taxes. Most people would be inclined to pay cash with the $300,000 they walked away with from up north after real estate commissions and closing costs. Then you would have no cash left over and of course no payment. But, you have permanently marooned $300,000 in your home which is not able to be touched until you move, sell or pass away. It cannot be used for anything other than an entry on your net worth page. However, you have 2 other options—assume you are

62— forward mortgage and reverse mortgage. On a forward mortgage, you could put down 60,000 and finance the other $240,000. The payments will total $412,000 (plus your down payment) at $1145 per month and you will make your last payment at 92. You will have moved almost a half million from bucket 1 or bucket 2 to equity in bucket 3. Or you could do what is called an H4P (HECM for Purchase). At 62 you will need about 60% down which is about 180,000. The other 120,000 is provided by your HECM lender and of course, payments are optional and not due until you have permanently moved out. Now think about the dramatic effect that has on your housing expense for the rest of your life! Your taxes and insurance have gone down and your payment went to zero. You also are able to have another $120,000 to invest with your other retirement funds and it is likely there will still be some equity left to pass on after you are gone to your children. But if there isn't, that is ok, because you have had a place to live— your dream retirement home for 10-20 maybe even 30 years and you only paid $180,000 one time. All the other payments are being paid for by the potential equity in the new home with no risk of paying more if home values don't keep pace.

But what if you need to upsize? Most people don't realize that 30% of baby boomers are buying larger or more expensive houses. This is partly because they are following their children (maybe more likely grandchildren!) to more expensive areas. So let's say someone in Wisconsin sells their paid off home for $250,000 and moves to Denver. It is really hard to find $250,000 homes in Denver! But they do find a $400,000 home they like in a 55 plus community.   Most retirees then make the dangerous mistake of using all their cash from their previous home PLUS pull another $150,000 from their nest egg, OR take out a forward mortgage and now make payments for the rest of their lives. Neither makes solid financial sense. If they use an H4P at 62, they only need to bring their $250,000 from Wisconsin as a down payment and the other $150,000 comes from the reverse mortgage. Now they have upsized, are close to the grandchildren, and still have no monthly payments. Their nest egg is still intact and their income in retirement has not decreased!

Remember, as we have stated before, the biggest expense in retirement is housing and an H4P will dramatically decrease that housing expense. But perhaps the most important issue is retiring in the house you really want to live in!   We have always said— the most important house we will buy is our retirement house because we will spend the most time there. When we are working and raising a family, we spend less time actually living in our homes. Don't make the mistake of downsizing to a home that you really don't like for the last few decades of your life. Live where you want to live! And if the home is a more expensive home— it might just hold its value better and despite the negative amortizing interest, your heirs may end up with more and not less!

Delay Social Security

It is a potential tragedy that about half of retirees take their social security at sixty-two and sixty-three. If you die early— its a smart decision— if you live to life expectancy or your widow does—you shortchanged your retirement. The vast majority of those people drawing early, will live much longer than they are thinking when they make that decision. Let's take a quick look at Mike and Mary—real couple, names changed. If Mike takes his benefits at sixty-two, then he will receive $1,844 per month; at sixty-seven, he will receive $2,725 per month. If he waits until seventy, then he will receive $3,438 per month. If they have a $300,000 home that is mostly paid off at sixty-two, then they would receive almost $2,000 per month from a reverse mortgage from the time they turn sixty-two until seventy. If the house is not paid off, then they would probably be eliminating a mortgage payment, which is pretty close to that same amount. Mary could still take her social security if they wanted extra money early, and if Mike passed away before her, then she would receive his $3,438 check instead of her smaller amount.

Your social security payout is one of the most significant gears in your retirement financial machine. Don't shortchange yourself by taking it too early. This is a decision you must make with your financial advisor. There are many factors that go into when you start drawing. But once you start, you can't turn the clock back and do it differently. Most of the time, you will be better off waiting and not drawing at sixty-two. But that doesn't mean you have to delay your retirement. The reverse mortgage or your other assets can replace that income for a few years or up to eight years if you wait until sixty-seven or seventy.

There is some controversy over this concept. It is important to note: In late 2017, the CFPB published an article warning that claimed that reverse mortgages should not be used to delay social security. This was almost immediately followed by rebuttals from the financial planning community disagreeing with the premise and exposing some faulty math used by the CFPB writers. You can read both sides and make your own decision. My personal feeling is that the CFPB did a disservice to millions of seniors in commentary that continues to scare people into using reverse mortgages only as a loan of last resort.

https://www.consumerfinance.gov/about-us/newsroom/cfpb-report-warns-taking-out-reverse-mortgage-loan-can-be-expensive-way-maximize-social-security-benefits/

This is the last paragraph and the link from the Hopkins Forbes magazine article:

"In the end, CFPB's analysis is incredibly flawed, misleading, and harmful. They rush to amazingly general conclusions about an entire strategy based on one scenario, but even that scenario shows a benefit of the strategy if used correctly. The strategy itself is likely employed by less than .1% of the United States population, so one has to wonder why the CFPB is spending their time and taxpayers money on such an ill-conceived and misleading report. If anything, the strategy is probably vastly underutilized not over. Instead of driving American's away from a strategy

that the CFPB showed was viable, they should be looking to provide guidance and insight into how Americans can effectively use home equity, Social Security, and reverse mortgages in positive ways to improve their retirement security."

https://www.forbes.com/sites/jamiehopkins/2017/08/28/cfpb-releases-misleading-report-on-social-security-deferral-strategies/#2d02b2e13a1b

Mary Beth Franklin also weighed in on the report in an Investment News article:

*"The Consumer Financial Protection Bureau (CFPB) issued **a new report** warning seniors against using a reverse mortgage as an income bridge to delay collecting Social Security benefits. While the report rightly points outs the potential risks of reverse mortgages, it demonstrates little understanding of the nuances of Social Security claiming strategies and overstates the typical cost of a reverse mortgage in today's marketplace."*

http://www.investmentnews.com/article/20170906/BLOG05/170909967/reverse-mortgages-under-fire-again

So, the detailed research done by the financial-planning community appears to be much more accurate and detailed than the very basic argument from the CFPB. We highly recommend that you discuss this with a qualified financial planner who has read Wade Pfau's book and Jamie Hopkins' articles. Dr. Pfau and Dr. Hopkins and many in the industry are looking at the fact that widows having a larger income check in their eighties and nineties are better off than those that have a lot of equity. At that point, Medicaid is a safety net for those who have a long-term care need toward the end of their lives. Common sense says that if all of your equity is gone but you have a larger income, it is much easier to maintain your lifestyle and stay above the poverty line.

I would like to insert here the importance of working with an informed financial advisor. Ask them if they have read the research by these top people in the industry—John Salter, Barry Sacks, Jamie Hopkins and Wade Pfau. Some advisors just don't keep up with this cutting edge financial research on home equity and if they don't know about the research — quite frankly they are not in a position to advise you on your retirement. I recently had a financial advisor working with a client planning to buy a home with the H4P and she consistently came up with basic objections which proved she knew nothing about the research. Her ego didn't allow her to want to learn about it either. Fortunately the client did not take her advice because it was simply wrong.

Pressure Off Bucket Two

It is more dangerous coming down a mountain than going up. It can also be more dangerous spending your money in retirement than it was trying to accumulate it. A term often used by financial advisors is *sequence of returns risk*. How and when you draw money out of any retirement asset determines how long your assets will last, which is often referred to as portfolio longevity. If you drew from your IRA in 2009 when the market crashed, then you would have locked in losses. However, if you had waited, the market would have restored a majority of those losses. Informed financial advisors like to use funds drawn from a reverse mortgage when other assets have taken a dip and the market is down. Then you can even use your gains to pay back some of the loan if you wish to create more cash availability and tax deductions down the road.

Save Money on Income Taxes

Paying income taxes in retirement is very common if you have more assets than just social security. Once you pay those taxes, that money is gone forever and cannot be recovered like a stock market loss can. Proceeds from a reverse mortgage are borrowed money, so they are tax free. Taking money from an IRA is taxed as ordinary income. Many other sources of income in retirement, including wages if you're still working, are also taxable. Many retirees use reverse mortgage proceeds to reduce their taxable income and thus the amount of taxes they pay. They also use it to pay taxes on Roth conversions if it makes sense from a tax perspective to pay now rather than later.

A really exciting aspect of the reverse mortgage is that you are able to get a potential tax deduction on interest and mortgage insurance when you make a payment. A regular mortgage has to be paid monthly, but a reverse mortgage never requires payments; they are optional. You can let the interest accrue and then make payments when there is a larger amount that is deductible. You decide when, if ever, to make payments when it is advantageous to your tax situation. You will lose no options for home interest deduction options and will likely gain more flexibility.

We discussed in the previous chapter that even if you never make payments, then your children might have the ability to take a tax deduction when they inherit your house after you pass away. That can potentially allow you to pass a greater portion of your estate, tax free, to the next generation.

Tax law is complex, and you must consult a tax advisor who understands how deductions work in regard to reverse mortgages. Tom Davison offers a great resource to share with your advisor.

https://toolsforretirementplanning.com/2015/12/03/ save-taxes/

Life Insurance and Long-Term Care Insurance

Home Health Care $45,760 Annually		Assisted Living Facility $43,539 Annually		Nursing Home Care $92,378 Annual (Private)	
•	Alzheimer's Care	•	Private Apartments	•	Full-time In Facility Care
•	Meal Prep / Diet Monitoring	•	On Site Nursing	•	Advanced LTC
•	Light Housekeeping	•	Help With Daily Living	•	Therapy, Rehabilitation, Medication
•	Errands Or Shopping	•	Help With Medication	•	Skilled 24 Hour Nursing

Medicaid Only Pays for Shared Rooms

• 95 % of People Have no LTC Insurance

• Over 50% Will Need LTC Insurance

• Data from 2016 survey, conducted by Carescout base on 15,000 surveys

I could write a whole book on the dangers of long-term care expenses and the proper use of life insurance in legacy planning. Let's condense this down to a simple example. Joe and Ellen are paying more than $1,200 a month for their mortgage and will be for another twenty years. If they did a reverse mortgage to eliminate that payment and instead invested that same amount monthly in life insurance with long-term care riders, then they would kill two birds with one stone. They would create a legacy of somewhere between $600,000 to $700,000 in a death benefit to replace their much smaller home value, and they would also be able to access part of the death benefit for long-term care protection if they needed it before they passed away. Now, I just oversimplified a whole lot of issues and made some assumptions. They still have to qualify for the life insurance. But assuming they could—as millions of baby boomers can—imagine the effect that this would have on private funding of long-term care and larger legacies to pass to the next generation.

It is estimated that over 50 percent of baby boomers will need some sort of long-term care before they pass away. Those costs are not funded by Medicare or any regular health insurance policy. That has to come out of other retirement funds. The experts agree that with only 5 percent of baby boomers holding long-term care insurance, there is a crisis on the horizon that cannot be covered by Medicaid or any other government program. There is simply not enough money there. This is a topic very near and dear to my heart because I've experienced this personally as well as professionally. Don't make the mistake of not planning for this huge issue. Use some of that $6 trillion home equity bucket to deal with this problem.

But Ernie says, "I will let the government take care of long-term care. I paid a lot of taxes, and that's one way that I'll get the money back at the end." This is not a good thought process, Ernie! First, Medicaid is a poverty program, and you have to be broke or look like you're broke to collect. That's not the goal for most of us. But here's the really big issue. If all the baby boomers think this way, then there will be a lot of Ernies needing to be taken care of ten or fifteen years from now, and I shudder to think of what kind of care Ernie will get when millions of others are needing long-term care all at the same time. I think I'll make plans to pay for my own!

Standby Line of Credit

But Carol says, "We have plenty of money. Our $500,000 home is paid off. We have a big IRA, we are one of the lucky ones who have pensions, and Jim is still working. We have more money than we need." I have heard this hundreds of times!

I have two answers for Jim and Carol. First, if you have more money than you need, then you should start giving it away, including the equity in your home. You can help your church, a charity, or your family. One of our clients who is worth over $4 million took all his available home equity and systematically gave it to his heirs so that he could enjoy the giving while he was alive with a warm hand instead of waiting to give with a cold hand. (Remember that any gifts during a Medicaid five-year lookback period can affect your eligibility for Medicaid long-term care benefits.)

The second answer for Jim and Carol would especially apply if they were in their sixties. The only thing certain about the future is that it's uncertain. The best time to set up a line of credit is when you don't need it. They would be eligible for an initial $200,000 line of credit in their sixties and it will be worth $400,000 in their seventies, and by the time they get to their late eighties, it will be worth over $800,000. You never know what lies ahead or when there will be a rainy day. As we said before, the best time to get an umbrella is when it's not raining. Set up a reverse line of credit while you can qualify and before you need it, regardless of how much money you have. I think there is a country song that says you can't have too much money, and you can't have too much fun. I would say that there's some truth to that—that is, if you want to live happily ever after!

Have Some Fun: Check Off the Bucket List

The last recommendation has nothing to do with dying with the most money, getting the best rate of return, increasing your assets, or following the right sequence of returns. Some things you can't place a dollar value on. When you have worked your whole life to get to the point of retirement, sometimes working sixty- to seventy-hour weeks, raising your children, changing careers, being downsized, working second jobs, starting a business, and going through all the trials and tribulations of life, maybe it's time to do some fun and memorable things. I don't think Cinderella felt bad about being the Prince's wife after all her hard work earlier in life!

There is a tragedy I have viewed many times. Parents worked very hard to fill bucket two and to send the money over to bucket three to pay off the house. They were always planning to buy a sports car or a motorcycle, go on a cruise, complete that mission trip, help a grandson with college, and achieve many other hopes and dreams. But they didn't spend any of the money because they kept it all, including their home equity, in the just-in-case reserve funds. And then they died, and the kids did all those things without them. Worse yet, they got sick before they died and all their money went to health care the last 2-3 years because they had no insurance.

Having a better retirement is not about having the highest net worth, the most money left at the end, or the biggest life insurance policy. It's certainly not about dying with a paid-off house with a ton of equity locked up inside it. But it is about being good stewards and properly *using* that money and equity you have accumulated. It is also about creating memories and doing significant things. On your deathbed, you will not be going down a financial statement and reviewing your net worth, but you will be remembering the memories that you created with your loved ones. At that point, no amount of money could replace the love and time that you shared together. So make decisions today so that when you are on your deathbed, you can say, "I really did live, after I got to retirement, happily ever after!"

Appendix 1: Financial-Planning and Reverse Mortgage Resources

Tools for Retirement Planning, March 30. Accessed May 22, 2017. https://toolsforretirementplanning.com/2014/03/30/income-tax-planning-with-a-reverse-mortgage/.

Davison, Tom. 2014. "Recovering a Lost Tax Deduction: April 2016 Update." Tools for Retirement Planning, December 14. Accessed May 21, 2017. https://toolsforretirementplanning.com/2015/12/14/recover-lost-tax-deduction/.

Davison, Tom. 2014. "Reverse Mortgage Funds Social Security Delay." Tools for Retirement Planning, March 31. Accessed May 22, 2017. https://toolsforretirementplanning.com/2014/03/31/ss-delay/.

Davison, Tom. 2014. "Reverse Mortgages: How Large Will a Line of Credit Be?" Tools for Retirement Planning, July 19. Accessed May 22, 2017. https://toolsforretirementplanning.com/2014/07/19/how-large-is-a-rm-loc/.

Davison, Tom. 2014. "Strategic Uses of Reverse Mortgages for Affluent Clients." Tools for Retirement Planning, April 16. Accessed May 22, 2017. https://toolsforretirementplanning.com/2014/04/16/reverse-mortgage-highlights/.

August 2016 Update, Reverse Mortgage Tax Deductions August 1. Accessed May 22, 2017. https://toolsforretirementplanning.com/2016/08/01/tax-deductions-and-reverse-mortgages-august-2016-update/.

Davison, Tom, and Keith Turner. 2015. "The Reverse Mortgage: A Strategic Lifetime Income Planning Resource." *Journal of Retirement* 3 (2): 61–79.

Giordano, Shelley. 2016. "An Alternative Asset to Buffer Sequence-of-Return Risk in Retirement." *Retirement Management Journal* 6 (1): 17–26.

Johnson, David W., and Zamira S. Simkins. 2014. "Retirement Trends, Current Monetary Policy, and the Reverse Mortgage Market." *Journal of Financial Planning* 27 (3): 52–5.

Kitces, Michael. 2011. "Evaluating Reverse Mortgage Strategies." *The Kitces Report.* Accessed May 22, 2017. https://www.kitces.com/prior-newsletters/.

Kitces, Michael. 2011. "A Fresh Look at the Reverse Mortgage." *The Kitces Report.* Accessed May 22, 2017. https://www.kitces.com/prior-newsletters/.

Kitces, Michael. 2013. "Is a Reverse Mortgage Better Than Keeping a Traditional Amortizing Mortgage in Retirement?" *Nerd's Eye View*, September 18. Accessed May 22, 2017. https://www.kitces.com/blog/is-a-reverse-mortgage-better-than-keeping-a-traditional-amortizing-mortgage-in-retirement/.

Kitces, Michael. 2013. "Taking a Fresh Look at Reverse Mortgages in Retirement." American Institute of CPAs. Accessed May 22, 2017. http://www.aicpa.org/InterestAreas/

PersonalFinancialPlanning/CPEAndEvents/Pages/Reverse-Mortgage.aspx.

Pfau, Wade D. 2014. "The Hidden Value of a Reverse Mortgage Standby Line of Credit." *Advisor Perspectives*, December 9. Accessed May 22, 2017. https://www.advisor-perspectives.com/articles/2014/12/09/the-hidden-value-of-a-reverse-mortgage-standby-line-of-credit.

Pfau, Wade D. 2015. "Advisors Need A Fresh Look At Reverse Mortgages. Accessed May 22, 2017. https://www.advisorperspectives.com/articles/2015/12/01/advisors-need-a-fresh-look-at-reverse-mortgages.

Pfau, Wade D. 2016. "Incorporating Home Equity into a Retirement Income Strategy." *Journal of Financial Planning* 29 (4): 41–9.

Pfau, Wade D. 2016. "Understanding the Line of Credit Growth for a Reverse Mortgage." *Journal of Financial Planning*, 37–9. https://www.onefpa.org/journal/Pages/MAR16-Understanding-the-Line-of-Credit-Growth-for-a-Reverse-Mortgage.aspx.

Pfeiffer, Shaun C., Angus Schaal, and John Salter. 2014. "HECM Reverse Mortgages: Now or Last Resort?" *Journal of Financial Planning* 27 (5): 44–51.

Pfeiffer, Shaun C., John Salter, and Harold Evensky. 2013. "Increasing the Sustainable Withdrawal Rate Using the

Standby Reverse Mortgage." *Journal of Financial Planning* 26 (12): 55–62.

Sacks, Barry H., Nicholas Maningas Sr., Stephen R. Sacks, and Francis Vitagliano. 2016. "Recovering a Lost Deduction." *Journal of Taxation* 124 (4): 157–69.

Sacks, Barry H., and Stephen R. Sacks. 2012. "Reversing the Conventional Wisdom: Using Home Equity to Supplement Retirement Income." *Journal of Financial Planning* 25 (2): 43–52.

Salter, John, Shaun Pfeiffer, and Harold Evensky. 2012. "Standby Reverse Mortgages: A Risk Management Tool for Retirement Distributions." *Journal of Financial Planning* 25 (8): 40–8.

Tomlinson, Joe. 2014. "How Reverse Mortgages Improve Sustainable Withdrawal Rates." *Advisor Perspectives*, March 18. Accessed May 22, 2017. https://www.advisorper-spectives.com/articles/2014/03/18/how-reverse-mortgag-es-improve-sustainable-withdrawal-rates.pdf.

Tomlinson, Joe. 2015. "New Research: Reverse Mortgages, SPIAs and Retirement Income." *Advisor Perspectives*, April 14. Accessed May 22, 2017. https://www.advisorperspec-tives.com/articles/2015/04/14/new-research-reverse-mort-gages-spias-and-retirement-income.

Tomlinson, Joe, Shaun Pfeiffer, and John Salter. 2016. "Reverse Mortgages, Annuities and Investments: Sorting Out the Options to Generate Sustainable Retirement Income." *Journal of Personal Finance* 15 (1): 27–36.

Wagner, Gerald C. 2013. "The 6.0 Percent Rule." *Journal of Financial Planning* 26 (12): 46–54.

Wagner, Gerald C. 2014. "Consider a HECM Reverse Mortgage Now." Accessed May 22, 2017. https://tcbdavison.files.wordpress.com/2014/06/consider_a_hecm_reverse_mortgage_now_v4.pdf.

Appendix 2: Resources on How Reverse Mortgages Work

Giordano, Shelley. 2015. *What's the Deal with Reverse Mortgages?* Pennington, NJ: People Tested Media.

Hultquist, Dan. 2016. *Understanding Reverse 2016. Answers to Common Questions—Simplifying the New Reverse Mortgage.* Seattle: CreateSpace.

Munnell, Alicia H., and Steven A. Sass. 2014. "The Government's Redesigned Reverse Mortgage Program." Center for Retirement Research at Boston College. Accessed May 21, 2017. http://crr.bc.edu/wp-content/uploads/2014/01/IB_14-1_508x.pdf.

Pfau, Wade. 2016. *Reverse Mortgages: How to Use Reverse Mortgages to Secure Your Retirement.* McLean, VA: Retirement Research Media.

Sass, Steven, Alicia H. Munnell, and Andrew Eschtruth. 2014. "A Retirement Planning Guide: Using Your House for Income in Retirement." Center for Retirement Research at Boston College. Accessed May 21, 2017. http://crr.bc.edu/wp-content/uploads/2014/09/c1_your-house_final_med-res.pdf.

Backman, Maurie. 2017. "10 Retirement Stats That Will Blow You Away." *The Motley Fool*, April 16. Accessed May

21, 2017. https://www.fool.com/retirement/2017/04/16/10-retirement-stats-that-will-blow-you-away.aspx.

Davison, Tom. 2017. "Tax Deductions and Reverse Mortgages: April 2017 Update." Tools for Retirement Planning, April 18. Accessed May 22, 2017. https://toolsforretirement-planning.com/2017/04/18/tax-deductions-and-reverse-mortgages-april-2017-update/.

Ellis, Charles D., Alicia H. Munnell, and Andrew D. Eschtruth. 2014. *Falling Short: The Coming Retirement Crisis and What to Do about It*. New York: Oxford University Press.

Giordano, Shelley. 2015. *What's the Deal with Reverse Mortgages?* Pennington, NJ: People Tested Media.

Gladwell, Malcolm. 2000. *The Tipping Point: How Little Things Can Make a Big Difference*. New York: Little, Brown.

Hopkins, Jamie. 2015. "Reverse Mortgages Can Be a Retiree's Saving Grace." *Forbes*, October 7. Accessed May 21, 2017. https://www.onereversemortgage.com/wp-content/uploads/2016/04/Reverse-Mortgages-Can-Be-a-Retirees-Saving-Grace.pdf.

Hultquist, Dan. 2017. *Understanding Reverse 2017: Answers to Commons Questions—Simplifying the New Reverse Mortgage*. Seattle: CreateSpace.

Kadlec, Dan. 2016. "Retirees' Biggest Asset May Be Hiding in Plain Sight." *TIME*, April 4.

Kotlikoff, Laurence J., and Scott Burns. 2004. *The Coming Generational Storm: What You Need to Know about America's Economic Future*. Cambridge, MA: MIT Press.

Kotlikoff, Laurence J., and Scott Burns. 2012. *The Clash of Generations: Saving Ourselves, Our Kids, and Our Economy*. Cambridge, MA: MIT Press.

Lieber, Ron. 2014. "Parents, the Children Will Be Fine. Spend Their Inheritance Now." *The New York Times*, September 19. Accessed May 22, 2017. https://www.nytimes.com/2014/09/20/your-money/estate-planning/parents-the-children-will-be-fine-spend-their-inheritance-now.html?_r=1.

Osterland, Andrew. 2017. "Cash-Strapped Seniors: Weigh Reverse-Mortgage Pros, Cons." *CNBC*, April 21. Accessed May 21, 2017. http://www.cnbc.com/2017/04/21/reverse-mortgages-can-be-a-boon-for-cash-strapped-seniors.html.

Pfau, Wade D. 2015. "Advisors Need a Fresh Look at Reverse Mortgages." *Advisor Perspectives*, December 1. Accessed May 21, 2017. https://www.advisorperspectives.com/articles/2015/12/01/advisors-need-a-fresh-look-at-reverse-mortgages.

Pfau, Wade D. 2016. "Incorporating Home Equity into a Retirement Income Strategy." *Journal of Financial Planning* 29 (4): 41–9.

Pfau, Wade D. 2016. *Reverse Mortgages: How to Use Mortgages to Secure Your Retirement*. McLean, VA: Retirement Research Media.

Sacks, Barry H., Nicholas Maningas Sr., Stephen R. Sacks, and Francis Vitagliano. 2016. "Recovering a Lost Deduction." *Journal of Taxation*. https://tcbdavison.files.wordpress.com/2016/04/sacks-et-al-recovering-a-lost-deduction-in-journal-of-taxation-april-2016.pdf.

US Department of State. 2005. "2005 State of the Union Address." Accessed May 21, 2017. https://2001-2009.state.gov/r/pa/ei/wh/rem/41479.htm.

Wikipedia. 2017. "Cinderella." Last modified May 20. Accessed May 21, 2017. https://en.wikipedia.org/wiki/Cinderella.

Made in the USA
Columbia, SC
17 January 2018